TAG, TOSS & RUN

40 CLASSIC LAWN GAMES

Paul Tukey & Victoria Rowell

Storey Publishing

The mission of Storey Publishing is to serve our customers by
publishing practical information that encourages
personal independence in harmony with the environment.

Edited by Carleen Madigan and Lisa H. Hiley
Art direction by Alethea Morrison
Book design by woolypear
Text production by Jennifer Jepson Smith

Photography credits appear on page 204
Cover and primary game illustrations by © Adam McCauley
Additional spot illustrations by woolypear

Indexed by Christine R. Lindemer, Boston Road Communications

Storey Publishing
210 MASS MoCA Way
North Adams, MA 01247
www.storey.com

Printed in the United States by Versa Press
10 9 8 7 6 5 4 3 2 1

LIBRARY OF CONGRESS CATALOGING-IN-PUBLICATION DATA

Tukey, Paul.
  Tag, toss & run / by Paul Tukey and Victoria Rowell.
    p. cm.
  Includes index.
  ISBN 978-1-60342-560-5 (pbk. : alk. paper)
  1. Games—Juvenile literature. 2. Outdoor games—Juvenile literature. I. Rowell, Victoria. II. Title.
GV1203.T85 2012
790.1922—dc23
                              2011049410

Dedication

*To Dad and Marny and the Lessels family for keeping those lawn
games alive and well in our lives for all these years*

— P. T.

*To my loving children, Maya and Jasper, and my foster mother,
Agatha Wooten Armstead, for raising me on Forest Edge, our
60-acre farm in West Lebanon, Maine, where she introduced me
to so many fun backyard games, with laughter, love, and patience*

— V. R.

Contents

Introduction

*The American people cannot fail to welcome
a new book on play. Throughout our country there
is a growing appreciation of its importance
and its necessity during childhood and youth . . .
no child can develop normally unless he has
opportunities for a large amount of diversified play.*

— **Michael Vincent O'Shea**
Director of Education,
University of Wisconsin

We would like to believe that statement is as true as if it were spoken yesterday. But when Professor Michael Vincent O'Shea, the esteemed director of education at the University of Wisconsin, penned the above words in 1910, he could not possibly have contemplated that children's "play" would come to be defined by computer and video games as much as by balls, bats, or hide-and-seek.

As authors of this book on children's games, we have traveled the world on vastly disparate personal and public voyages. One of us has been a dancer, an actress, and an author, the other a sportswriter turned lawn care professional and magazine publisher. The common ground that fostered our collective dreams, however, was rural Maine in the 1960s. From one-room schoolhouses where the desks still had inkwells to fuzzy black-and-white televisions (if our families owned one at all) to party-line systems where neighbors took turns on their telephones (if they could afford one), ours was a world almost unimaginable to scores of children a half century later.

Without Game Boys or Nintendos or Wiis, and without iPods, iPhones, or instant messaging, life then probably sounds bleak to today's youth. But, oh, what fun we had! Our entire childhoods — spent with nothing more than our own wits and the loveable nitwits and nincompoops from our neighborhoods — were filled with endless outdoor games. Imagine this: our caregivers sent us through the front door in the morning with a sandwich in a brown bag and a canteen full of well water, but no cell phone, no pocket money, and, furthermore, no instructions other than to be home by dinnertime!

It wasn't that the adults in our lives didn't care about us. Quite the opposite. In our cases, however, they had farms to run, with long lists of chores, of which we were expected to do our share. When we were fin-ished cooking, cleaning, and making our beds, the adults felt absolutely no responsibility to fill in our free time. And, as we discovered about each other, we both lived in an economic reality where store-bought toys and games were a rare privilege, not a right. It was as if the Grinch had come by to swipe our galooks and our great big electro-who-cardio-shnoox — and never brought them back!

But just as Christmas still comes in the fabled Dr. Seuss classic, we still found our fun each day. Yes, we were poor, but we truly never knew it. If you recall gathering frog spawn in a jam jar, trapping a salamander under a tuna can or, we admit it, swiping the occasional bird's egg from a nest, you recall what we mean by fun. If you know the term "jacking for worms" or the thrill of catching fireflies in a jar at night, you know that the natural world holds more wonders than any megastore.

You may know that. But do your children?

"For a new generation, nature is more abstraction than reality. Increasingly, nature is something to watch, to consume, to wear — to ignore," wrote Richard Louv in *Last Child in the Woods,* the best-selling exposé about a phenomenon known as "nature deficit disorder" that explains children's disconnect with nature and all it represents.

The other issue, of course, is the physical and mental toll of a life lived in front of a computer and television. Obesity levels for 5- and 6-year-olds have doubled in the past decade and are even worse for teenagers. At least 10 percent of our kids have a diagnosed mental health problem ranging from attention deficit to hyperactivity to depression.

In bringing you this book, we are presenting a time-honored way for children to reconnect, not only with nature, but their communities, their comrades, their families, and their sense of self. In *Tag, Toss & Run,* we explore and perhaps introduce classic outdoor games in hopes that you will enjoy them with your children and teach your children to play them on their own. Whether played in your backyard, a public park, or in the paved nook of a cul-de-sac, these games, for children and the young at heart of all ages, are timeless treasures that — if you let them — will work their magic on your sons and daughters in the same way they might have nurtured you.

We think this book is at once timely and necessary, but it's also a rollicking nostalgic ride for parents and grandparents who remember simpler, healthier times. As we recalled the playground and backyard games of our own childhoods, we laughed out loud at our own memories and relived some silly old fears of games that we originally found intimidating. We fondly recollected the exhilaration of being selected as captain, with the privilege of first pick. We chuckled at those common, old anxieties about swinging and missing, tripping awkwardly on the jump rope, or finishing last in a race. Those moments made the home runs and blue-ribbon finishes all the sweeter.

In presenting a book on mostly old-fashioned outdoor games in this day and age, we have to acknowledge that some parents, caregivers, school administrators, and even sociologists will take issue with our list. Five of the games we selected are also included in a rather notorious publication known as "The Hall of Shame Games."

"The games included in the Hall of Shame have no business being played on a school playground and should be banned," says the list's creator, Professor Neil Williams of Eastern Connecticut State College, who has a doctorate in the instruction of physical education. "Some of the games have the potential to embarrass a student in front of his classmates, or to only celebrate the achievements of the truly gifted athletes.

These games focus on the elimination of students from the contest. And some of these games are flat-out dangerous."

But we're more inclined to agree with Christina Hoff Sommers, author of *One Nation Under Therapy: How the Helping Culture is Eroding Self-Reliance.* "The good intentions or dedication of the self-esteem educators are not in question, but their common sense is," she writes. "With few exceptions, the nation's children are mentally and emotionally sound. They relish the challenge of high expectations. They can cope with red pens, Tug of War and Dodge Ball. They can handle being 'It.'"

So be forewarned. We've included dodgeball, kickball, and Red Rover in our book. Not to mention British bulldogs, tug of war, and other games where children can suffer scrapes, bumps, and bruised psyches. Our view is not "danger be damned" and we certainly believe that no child should ever be forced to play any game at any time against his or her will. We also strongly believe children and their caregivers need to know these games, try them together at first, and then make their own decisions about whether to allow the children to play again.

Surely even Professor Williams would agree to that. We know Professor O'Shea did! Play — real play outdoors on the lawn — is probably even more important now than it was a century ago.

Who Goes First?

Choosing captains, picking sides, and deciding who goes first is part of many backyard games. Here are a few time-honored methods for settling the question.

FLIP OF A COIN

Heads or tails? A tried-and-true, easy way to get a game started but perhaps the least interesting.

ROCK, PAPER, SCISSORS

A game unto itself, with its own world championship and an entry in *Guinness World Records 2012* (6,500 players at once), Rock, Paper, Scissors is played with hand gestures of a fist (rock), two fingers (scissors) and open palm (paper). In a game of two players vying for captaincy, the rock trumps scissors, the paper beats rock and the scissors cuts the paper. If both players "throw" the same gesture, they play again.

HAND OVER HAND

Using a stick or, especially, a baseball bat, one player tosses the object to the other, who must catch the stick or bat no higher than halfway up. The would-be captains then alternate grabbing the object just above each other's clenched fists until one player reaches the top and can stretch his or her thumb over the top of the stick or bat.

COUNTING OFF

In counting-off contests, one player recites a rhyme while pointing at a different player for each word in the rhyme. A classic example is, "One potato, two potato, three potato, four; five potato, six potato, seven potato, more; one big bad spud." Whoever is being pointed at during the word "spud" is the "it" player for that game.

Another traditional rhyme is "Eeny, meeny, miney, mo; catch a tiger by the toe. If he hollers, let him go. Eeny, meeny, miney, mo."

A CONTEST: ROTTEN EGG

This one can be a footrace or a throwing challenge. The slowest runner or shortest thrower becomes the "it" player.

WHICH HAND?

This straightforward contest involves hiding a pebble or other small object in one hand behind your back and having another player guess which hand. A correct selection wins the captaincy for that game.

DRAWING STRAWS

Another time-honored selection process, drawing straws is probably as old as, well, straw. Count out blades of grass or slender twigs for each person in the game, making sure one is noticeably shorter than the others. One player holds the straws in a fist, obscuring the ends, and each player draws one. The "it" player is the one who draws the shortest piece.

VOLLEY FOR SERVE

This is most often used in badminton, sepak takraw, and other net games that involve an initial serve to get the game going. A starting volley — which usually has to last for at least three consecutive successful hits across the net — is used to determine who goes first, or in some cases who is team captain.

Calling All Players

A t the end of any game that involves hiding and seeking (see Capture the Flag or Kick the Can, for example), a call goes out to all players who are still hiding, telling them to come back to home base. Whether that call is "olly olly oxen free," "ally ally in come free," or one of any number of variations seems to depend on where you live, though "olly olly in come free" seems to be the most common current usage.

The origin is unclear but most sources claim the phrase derives from "all ye, all ye outs in free" or words to that effect, meaning that the game is over and players who haven't been found can come in without being caught, either to start another round or to go home to supper.

The word "oxen" has nothing to do with cattle; it is thought to be a childish corruption of "outs in." Some note the similarity to the German phrase "Alle, alle auch sind frei," which means "everyone, everyone is also free." Whatever the origin, this phrase has long been heard ringing out through neighborhoods and playgrounds and we hope it continues to do so!

BACKYARD GOLF

Although it originally barely resembled the modern game in which players with metal clubs launch a small white ball toward tiny holes hundreds of yards away, golf has been enjoyed by players of all ages for centuries. Some serious players go to the extreme of installing putting greens in their lawns. Others dig sand pits so they can practice blasting balls to their heart's content.

Stepping on a real public golf course, even a miniature golf course, for the first time can be an intimidating experience; gaining some

THE SETUP

BASIC IDEA
Hit the ball in the hole using the fewest strokes possible

PLAYING AREA
Smooth, short grass is best

EQUIPMENT
• Clubs — putters are good; small ones are available for younger players
• A few golf balls
• A variety of targets (buckets, lawn furniture, branches — use your imagination!) to make a course

AGES
5 and up

PLAYERS
1 or more

confidence at home is a great first step. Those tight backyard confines become a great equalizer that allows a grandfather to teach the basics of the game to a grandchild or for siblings to engage in a little friendly competition.

No Fairway Required

You don't need elaborate equipment and precision grooming to have fun in your own backyard. A club and a ball and some closely cropped grass with a few targets or obstacles are all that's required for a friendly game. The possibilities for establishing a mini-golf obstacle course at home are endless — through the swing set, under the picnic table, around the oak tree, and in the "hole," which can be any size container turned on its side, from as big as a bucket to as tricky as a tennis-ball can.

Rules. On the surface, golf is incredibly straightforward: The player taking the fewest number of shots to hit the ball into a hole or series of holes is the winner. On a conventional golf course, all sorts of other rules and etiquette come into play; golfers are huge on etiquette! But on a miniature course, pretty much the only

15

rule is "hit the ball in the hole." If it doesn't roll in, hit it again. Players can determine if each one takes a turn at each hole or one person plays the whole course before the next player goes.

Strategy. Becoming a good putter takes lots of practice and the acquired ability to "read" the green or putting surface. That means you need to judge how hard to hit the ball given the thickness and height of the grass or mat, or how much the surface angles and undulates between the ball and the hole. When hitting or stroking a putt, some players will look at the hole, but the best advice is to keep your eye on the ball and your head steady until the head of the putter has made contact with the ball. That will give you the best chance of hitting the ball where you want it to go.

16

The first miniature golf courses in the United States began to appear at luxury hotels in the late 1800s.

«FLASHBACK PAUL«

I've long had a love–hate relationship with golf. Although Arnold Palmer was popular when I was young, boys of my age never seemed to be encouraged to play his game. When my older friends Skip and Stan talked me into playing golf in my mid-20s, I wished I had started sooner so that I could have played better. Then, as I aged and had children of my own, I never seemed to have time to play and never played very well when I did.

That's why miniature golf is such a great game. With little practice or training, and with limited time, anyone can putt a ball toward a hole. Whether it's through a pirate cove at a putt-putt course or around an undulation in your own lawn, it's a great way to enjoy the outdoors.

Variation: Big Birdie Golf

Implements for golf are some of the most common items registered with the U.S. Patent and Trademark Office, and numerous manufacturers have come up with variations on the golf theme as backyard, beach, and tailgate games. One

Guinness World Records credits 66-year-old Gergus Muir with the longest successful putt in history. Having watched his two friends hit the ball over the par-3 fifth hole at the Eden Course at St Andrews in Scotland, Muir pulled his putter out of his bag. With a gale-force wind at his back, he gave the ball a mighty whack. Rolling along the fairway and onto the green, the ball came to rest in the hole — 125 yards away.

17

of our favorites is Big Birdie Golf, which features golf balls glued to the feathers of badminton-like birdies.

Players use their "wedge" clubs to lob the Big Birdie balls onto flat, netted targets set up 20 to 30 feet away. The game is scored like horseshoes, with balls closest to the center worth three points and balls on the outer ring worth one point. For young children not adept at swinging a golf club, the Big Birdie balls can be tossed underhand toward the target.

The Granddaddy of Golf Courses

Although both the Dutch and Chinese have evidence of stick-and-ball target games from 800 to 1,500 years old, the birthplace of the modern game is acknowledged to be St Andrews, a legendary course established in Scotland in 1400.

In 1867, St Andrews opened what is believed to be the world's first miniature golf course, the Himalayas, for women only.

Stone bridge and clubhouse of the Royal and Ancient Golf Club in St Andrews

BADMINTON

ALSO KNOWN AS
Battledore and
Shuttlecock,
Hanetsuki (Japan)

The world's second most popular sport (after soccer), badminton deserves a well-worn area in every summer yard. More so than tennis, badminton can be enjoyed by players of virtually all ages and abilities and it doesn't require a specially groomed lawn.

Because the birdie, or "shuttlecock," is small and unintimidating to hit with the lightweight racquets, badminton is a great starter game for children. At the highest levels of competition, however, the players are among the most fit and coordinated athletes in the world, and

THE SETUP

BASIC IDEA
2 to 4 players hit the
birdie over the net

PLAYING AREA
Flat, smooth grass
is best

EQUIPMENT
• A racquet for each
  player
• A birdie or two
• A net (a rope will do)

AGES
7 and up

PLAYERS
2 or 4

the birdie can come off the racquet at speeds exceeding 200 miles per hour.

Setting Up at Home

Played one against one or two against two, the official game calls for a court 20 feet wide and 44 feet long (approximately 6 by 13 meters). Smaller spaces near buildings work just fine because the shuttlecocks, which weigh only a few ounces, won't harm surrounding plants and property. Having two younger or less experienced players team up against one older one is a good way to balance out family play.

Rules. Badminton has pretty simple rules and the scoring is much easier than tennis. Games are commonly played to 11 or 15 points, but you can decide on any number. Some versions hold that a team must win by 2 points.

- The serving team hits the birdie from behind the end line over the net and into the opponents' court, and the opponents try to hit it back.

- If the birdie lands on the ground within the boundaries of the opponents' court, the serving team scores a point and retains service. The same player serves until losing a point.

- If the birdie hits the net and drops to the ground, or otherwise fails to land in bounds, no point is scored and the serving team loses the serve.

- If the opposing team returns the serve and the serving team fails to hit it back, no point is scored and the serve goes to the other team.

- A player or team must be serving to score.

- Only one player on each side may hit the birdie to return it.

21

Although most birdies available in stores are constructed of plastic and synthetic rubber, an official birdie is made from cork and goose feathers. Apparently, feathers from the left wing are best, with 16 needed for the perfect birdie.

Strategy. In singles games, being able to anticipate where the birdie will be hit is important because the court is quite large for one player to cover. In doubles, communication becomes vital because, although either player can hit the birdie, it can be hit only once before clearing the net. For friendly backyard games, of course, the court size can be adjusted to accommodate available space or the size and ability of the players.

Serving strategy can be a major factor in the outcome of the game. High, arching serves to the back of the opponent's court are difficult for the opponent to return as a winning shot. Lower, faster serves can sometimes catch opponents off guard and score "aces," which are serves that are not returned.

Badminton has been a popular family game and social pastime for quite a long time.

BATTLEDORE AND SHUTTLECOCK

This game earned its curious name from the Badminton estate in Gloucestershire, England. One summer day in 1873, the Duke of Beaufort, eager to show off his lawn to refined guests dressed in bonnets and top hats, staged a contest that featured a paddle known as a "battledore" and a feathered cork called a "shuttlecock."

Although the new "badminton game" borrowed heavily from games at least a thousand years old, its popularity soon spread across Great Britain and eventually to the United States, where the Badminton Health Club of Boston was founded in 1908.

Made in China

Badminton has been contested as an Olympic sport since 1992, in men's and women's singles and doubles and also in mixed doubles. The Far East has dominated the competitions, with China (30), Indonesia (18), and South Korea (17) winning by far the most medals in five Games.

Paul Erik Hoyer-Larsen of Denmark is the only competitor from outside that region to win the gold medal (Atlanta, Georgia, 1996), while the United States and Canada have never medaled.

BLIND MAN'S BUFF

ALSO KNOWN AS
Blind Man's Buff,
Blind Man's Wand,
La Galinita Ciega
(Mexico), La Gallina
Ciega (Spain),
Le Colin-Maillard
(France)

A variation on the classic game of tag, time-honored Blind Man's Bluff is a far less competitive version. Being more about socialization and camaraderie than winning and losing, the game has been played by kings and queens, monarchs and emperors, and little boys and girls who profess each other "icky," but would not-so-secretly like to get to know each other a little better. This is one game where members of the opposite sex are almost always welcome to participate no matter what age.

THE SETUP

BASIC IDEA
A blindfolded player
tries to catch others
who scatter, then
freeze in place

PLAYING AREA
Any open area,
even indoors

EQUIPMENT
A bandana or scarf

AGES
5 and up

PLAYERS
At least 3, but more fun
with a larger group

Catch Me If You Can

In some games, the first tagged player is automatically "it" and becomes the next blind man. In other versions, the blind man must find and tag all other players; however, in most cases, the blind man touches the first tagged player's face and body to identify him or her. A correct guess makes that player the next blind man, but an incorrect guess continues the game with the same blind man. It's the touching aspect of the game, innocent or otherwise, that has made Blind Man's Bluff a provocative subject for painters and poets for centuries.

Variation: Blind Man's Wand

Folks uncomfortable with the touching and poking inherent in the traditional game can play a more tepid variation called Blind Man's Wand that gives the "it" player something to hold such as a wooden spoon or rolled newspaper. After spinning around several times, with all the other players standing around in a circle, the blind man finds a player in the traditional way, but tags him or her with the object rather than his or her hand.

A GAME OF KINGS

Blind Man's Bluff reached its peak of popularity in the Tudor period in England that lasted from kings Henry VII and VIII through the reign of Elizabeth I (1485–1603).

A lovely painting titled "Blind Man's Buff," rendered in 1789 by the provocative artist Francisco de Goya y Lucientes, depicts members of the Italian aristocracy playing the game.

26

The blind man then makes nonverbal sounds, which must be imitated by the tagged player until the blind man guesses the identity of the player. If the blind man is correct, the tagged player is then "it;" if not, the game continues with the same blind man.

Rules. Something magical happens when you take away the sight of one of the players, who must then rely on hearing, touch, and smell to get by.

○ **The game begins when the blindfolded player, having been spun around while the others scatter, yells "Stop!"**

○ **All the other players must freeze in place.**

○ **The blind man says, "Blind man's . . . !"**

○ **All the other players must answer "bluff." The call and response is repeated until the blind man follows the sounds to tag and identify a player. That player becomes the next blind man.**

The command to stop requires that all players plant their feet, but that doesn't mean they can't contort their bodies, squat, bend, or otherwise try to avoid being tagged. This can be especially fun in the variations of the game that don't require vocal clues. Instead, the blind man wanders around the yard with his or her hands forward until he or she finds a player. The biggest challenge for the other players is to not giggle!

Strategy. Players can disguise their voices to avoid being tagged, especially if their best friend is the blind man. It's often a good idea to designate one person as the referee for two reasons: 1) to make sure that all players respond according to the rules, and 2) to make sure the blind man doesn't wander into trouble.

In American colonial times, children began Blind Man's Bluff with a call-and-response that has been repeated millions of times. As the blindfold is tied over the player's face, the other player asks, "How many horses has your father?"

The blind man answers, "Three." "What color are they?" asks another player, to which the blind man replies, "Black, white, and grey." All the players then respond loudly, "Turn around three times and catch whom you may."

27

BOCCE

ALSO KNOWN AS
Boules (France),
Lawn Bowling,
Pétanque (France), Ula
Maika (Hawaii)

Generally recognized as the oldest sport on earth, this game is depicted in a 7,000-year-old Egyptian tomb painting. A bowling lawn has been maintained continuously in Southampton, England, since 1299, and today bocce is enjoyed around the world both for its simplicity and its complexity. True bocce has one significant variation from real lawn "bowls" in that the balls in lawn bowling are slightly asymmetrical.

The folks who take this game seriously build perfectly level courts covered in compacted

29

THE SETUP

BASIC IDEA
Take turns rolling the balls; those closest to the target ball score

PLAYING AREA
Official layout is up to 90 feet by 13 feet, but any decent lawn will work for a friendly game

EQUIPMENT
• Eight dense wooden balls in two different colors
• One smaller ball, the pallino

AGES
4 and up

PLAYERS
2 to 8

stone dust or even crushed oyster shells. Players are allowed to bounce the balls off the sides of low walls to work angles, just as in billiards, or lob the balls in the air so that they literally land on top of other balls. Many players are highly skilled masters who compete for far more than beer and bragging rights.

Strictly for Fun

As a family lawn game, however, the satisfaction comes from simply having a game with flexible rules that players of all ages can easily enjoy. The playing surface matters little and, in fact, boundaries do not even need to be drawn. If a 90-year-old grandmother is playing with her 5-year-old granddaughter, a successful game can be played on any patch of relatively smooth grass.

The game consists of eight balls (the "bocces"), about the size of grapefruits, in two different colors, and one small ball (the "pallino"), about the size of a golf ball. The object is throw or roll the bocces as close as possible to the pallino. The balls that are closest at the end of each round are scored and the rounds continue until one team reaches a certain number of points.

30

Rules. Games often begin with an initial contest to see who can lob or roll a bocce closest to the pallino, which is set off at some distance. The winner goes first.

○ Teams take turns throwing their bocces at the pallino, with players on each team throwing in turn.

○ After all 8 bocces have been thrown, the team with the bocce closest to the pallino scores a point. In some versions, the team scores for every bocce that is closer to the pallino than the other team's closest one.

○ The winner of each frame or round goes first in the next one.

○ The player or team that scores an agreed-upon number of points first wins. Games can range from 7 to 13 points. In most games a player or team must have a two-point advantage before a winner is declared.

Scoring example:
The brown team has two balls closer to the pallino than the green team and scores two points.

Strategy. Throughout the game, players can try to hit either the pallino or opponents' balls to change its position; therefore, a shot that looks good initially may not end up scoring a point by the time everyone has rolled.

One tip on a soft lawn surface is to lob the ball underhand with backspin so that it will tend to stop when it lands, allowing you to better control your shot. If the lawn surface is uneven, bumpy, or pocked, rolling a ball accurately can be difficult.

" LEARN THE LINGO "

Bocce The large balls that are thrown at the pallino

Raffa (*also bombing or spocking*) A throw aimed at another bocce, with the intention of hitting it out of the way

Pallino (*also pallina or jack*) The small target ball

Punto A throw aimed at the pallino, with the intention of scoring a point

Volo An aerial throw aimed at another bocce

KISSING FANNY

An enduring bocce legend emerged in the 1860s in Lyon, France, when a local waitress allegedly offered to expose her derriere to the losers of a match, who were then obliged to kiss her bare buttocks in public. To this day bocce clubs often post a painting or picture of "Fanny" on their walls. Any time a patron loses a match without scoring a single point, thus committing a "Fanny," he or she must kiss the artwork as a mock penalty.

31

Player of the Years

Italian Umberto Granaglia is generally believed to be the greatest player of all time. Named "Player of the Twentieth Century" by the Confédération Mondiale des Sports de Boules, he won a record 13 world championships, 12 European championship titles, and 46 Italian national championships between 1957 and 1980. He passed away in December 2008.

Martinez, California, claims to be the bocce capital of the United States, with more than a thousand competitors involved in their leagues and entire neighborhoods that gather informally in backyards. The U.S. Bocce Federation estimates that there are about 25 million enthusiasts in the United States today.

Players of various nationalities while away the hours at a bocce court on Ellis Island, in this 1933 photo.

BRITISH BULLDOGS

ALSO KNOWN AS
Black Tom, Dog
& Deer, Hill Dill,
Octopus, Pom-
Pom-Pull-Away,
Rushing Bases

Versions of this contest, mentioned in the earliest literary references to games in the United States, have been played by children the world over for centuries. Because no equipment is needed, it cuts across all cultures, from the wealthiest schoolyards in the West to the poorest desert plains of Africa, and although it certainly rewards speed and quickness, British bulldogs also helps build allegiances and strategy skills.

This can be an especially fun game for coaches to introduce to the practice field in

THE SETUP

BASIC IDEA
Make it past the "bulldog" without being caught; tagged players become bull-dogs until only one is left

PLAYING AREA
Any large, open space free of tripping hazards

EQUIPMENT
Markers to denote the center line and two end lines

AGES
4 and up

PLAYERS
4 or more

place of more rigid running drills. Younger children will rejoice in trying to "keep away" from an adult playing the role of bulldog, or the coach can watch from the sidelines while the players have at it. Either way, the players get loads of agility and stamina exercises without even realizing that they're "working out."

How to Play

The object of the game is to make it from one end of the field to the other without get-ting tagged — or in some cases lifted or even tackled — by the "it" player or players known as the bulldogs. In Australia, testosterone-filled games feature full-on roughhousing where the bulldog player must wrestle runners

BULLDOG

OTHER PLAYERS

Initial setup

to the ground or else hold a player in the air long enough to declare, "British bulldogs 1, 2, 3!" In the United States and in many other nations, however, the most aggressive versions of the game have been largely relegated to history.

Rules. Parallel boundaries are usually designated 30 or more feet apart on the playing field; the more players, the larger the field, which can be marked by gloves, hats, cones, or other items.

- After the initial bulldog or "it" player is selected, he or she stands in the middle of the field and all the other players line up along one boundary line.

- The "it" player then calls out "Bulldog," or "Pom pom pull away," or "Hill dill, time to take the hill," depending on the nation and the neighborhood.

- All the players try to run past the bulldog without getting tagged.

- When players are tagged, they must stand still until all the other players have reached the opposite boundary.

- For the next round, the tagged players become teammates of the original bulldog. When "Bulldog" is called again, the new teammates also try to tag the runners as they race or sneak their way back to the original boundary.

This activity continues until the last player to be tagged by the ever-expanding pack of bulldogs is declared the winner. That player is usually the first bulldog for the next round.

Strategy. For slower runners, different strategies can be important in this game. Sometimes allegiances form where packs of players run closely together under the assumption that the bulldog won't be able to catch everyone and a few players can sneak through.

Banned in Britain

British bulldogs has been banned on many playgrounds in Great Britain, where tackling commonly replaced lifting or tagging, and many traditionalists are outraged, despite the occasional playground scrape. "You just can't rule out risk altogether and we shouldn't be wrapping children in cotton wool," said Laura Midgley, a school governor who launched the Campaign Against Political Correctness. "Some accidents are inevitable, but that doesn't mean we should stop children from playing."

HAVE A PICKLE

This game, like many older children's chase contests, has deep roots as a war game in which children emulated their fathers on the battlefields. The name of the earliest American version of British bulldogs, "Hill Dill," was originally derived from "taking the hill," a common battle reference, and the simple Dutch chase game of Pekel, which translates as "pickle." Dill pickles were extremely popular with early American settlers as a food that could be consumed year-round!

36

CAPTURE THE FLAG

ALSO KNOWN AS
Flag Raiding

A classic old-fashioned neighborhood war game, Capture the Flag is a wonderful way to bring groups of children and adults together for competitive strategy and exercise.

A staple of the Boy Scouts of America hand-book for more than 60 years, the game has evolved in recent years with the advent of cell phones and walkie-talkies, which allow teammates to provide information on opponents' positions behind the big pine tree or the neighbor's deck. For the purest game, however, electronic devices should be banned. That puts

THE SETUP

BASIC IDEA
Teams try to capture their opponent's flag while defending their own territory

PLAYING AREA
A wide-open area with room for lots of running is best; rocks and trees for base camps, jails, and hiding spots add to the fun.

EQUIPMENT
- A brightly colored flag or trophy
- A picnic table works great as a jail or base camp

AGES
5 and up

PLAYERS
Teams of 3 or more is ideal

the emphasis on watching and listening carefully, then making a mad dash when it looks like the coast is clear. Playing at night is great fun, when the dim light gives cover to your actions and it's so quiet you can hear your teammate's panting and the beating of your own heart.

Attack and Defend

Although the game can be modified any of a dozen ways, it's all based on the idea of snagging the other team's treasure — the "flag," which can be any object — and bringing it back safely to your team's territory without getting caught. The game definitely puts a high premium on speed, stamina, and teamwork.

Rules. Players are divided into two teams, but the player count need not be even. Two or three faster, older players might face off against a dozen younger ones, for example, just to make it interesting. The game is typically played with each team simultaneously defending its own flag while trying to steal the other team's, though a variation is to have one team raid while the other team protects.

○ Start by defining the team territories: Fences, houses, streets, creeks, and trails make good boundaries. Each territory needs a home base with a designated safe area around it and a jail (see Strategy). The game begins with the flag or trophy hung in plain sight near the home bases.

○ Usually some players from each team guard the flag while faster players are designated as attackers; the positions can be switched at any time.

○ Defending players are not allowed in their own safe area unless pursuing an attacker.

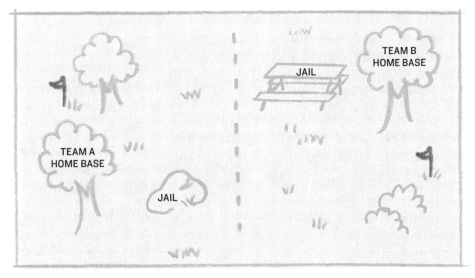

Suggested field of play

- Players who are tagged are either out of the game or put in jail.

- The first team to successfully grab the opposing flag and bring it back to their own territory wins.

Strategy. Deciding in advance what happens to captured players is a big part of the fun. They can either be eliminated for the rest of the game, or can be put in "jail" to be rescued by teammates who run swiftly into the opposing team's territory to tag them. Prisoners are not allowed to shout out instructions to other players on their team.

Players are usually allowed to rescue only one teammate at a time and a "no guard" zone is usually defined so that the guards can't simply sit right next to the flag for the entire game. The jail is set apart from the flag so that part of the challenge for the defenders is guarding the prisoners and the flag simultaneously.

The Boy Scouts of America play a version of this game using orienteering skills rather than running speed and hiding prowess. Troop leaders hide flags and give the starting points and compass bearings to the teams.

When a team finds its own flag, maps are provided to the opponent's flag. Reading a compass is a skill many of us were taught as children, but much of today's cell-phone generation might not have any idea that the needle always points north.

BATTLE CRY

Capture the Flag probably started in the United States during the Civil War when units of the Confederate and Union armies would mark their positions with flags. More than a third of the 1,520 Medals of Honor awarded during the war went to soldiers for either capturing the Confederate flag or for saving the 35-starred Union banner from the Confederates, who would have torn it to shreds.

How Big Was the Flag?

On September 19, 2009, coeds at Brigham Young University organized what is believed to be the largest game of Capture the Flag ever recorded, with 1,281 students running around a 40-acre golf course using glow lights to see at night. Although not officially recognized by the *Guinness World Records,* the game lasted more than 30 minutes; the blue team won but, most importantly, no one was injured.

The children of Civil War veterans may have based their games on tales brought home from the battlefield. Here Union soldiers capture a Confederate flag at the Battle of Murfreesboro.

CHEROKEE MARBLES

ALSO KNOWN AS
Digadayosdi,
Indian Marbles

Part golf and part croquet without the clubs or mallets, and somewhat similar to bocce, the game of Digadayosdi, otherwise known as Cherokee marbles, was played in this continent at least 800 years before the first European settlers landed at Jamestown and Plymouth Rock. Oddly enough, though, this team contest of skill, guile, memory, and patience never seemed to migrate outside the Cherokee Nation in what we now call Oklahoma.

"I have visited the Muscogee Creek Nation just across the Arkansas River from here and they have never heard of our game of marbles," said Phyllis Fife, the Director of Northeastern State University's Center for Tribal Studies. "Around here, though, it's been a fabric of the culture that has brought people of all ages together for centuries and to this day."

Family Fun

It's easy to see why Cherokee marbles has endured. Often played with six or seven players on each team, but sometimes with as many as a dozen, it's not uncommon to see children contesting shots with their grandparents. The skill comes in rolling the ball or "marble" accurately, and guile helps decide proper positioning throughout the game. Scores are never written down, so accurate recall is required, as is patience. The more players, the longer the game will last. The longer the game, the more the laughter, the debates, and the storytelling about hotly contested matches in the days of yore.

THEN AND NOW

Most places of worship in the Oklahoma Cherokee region were said to have once had an area set up for Cherokee marbles games — until the tribal elders realized that many players never made it inside for the service. The Cherokee Nation still holds an annual Cherokee marbles tournament on Labor Day weekend in Tahlequah, Oklahoma. The event gives far-flung Cherokee families and friends throughout the West a chance to reunite.

43

THE SETUP

BASIC IDEA
Be the first to roll a large "marble" so that it comes to rest in a series of shallow holes

PLAYING AREA
A large, flat surface that allows the marbles to roll smoothly; slight hills add an extra challenge. Gravel roads and pathways can also work.

EQUIPMENT
A pool or billiard ball for each player; field hockey and lacrosse balls work too, and golf balls can be used in a pinch.

AGES
5 and up

PLAYERS
6 to 20+, but an equal number on each team

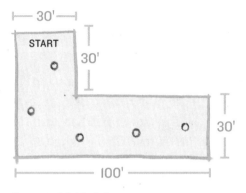

Suggested field of play

Note: *A common bulb planter is the perfect tool for setting up the field or course for a Cherokee marbles game. The resulting plugs of turf can be set aside while the game is played, and then reinserted into the lawn so that the holes don't cause unsightly tripping hazards.*

Rules. The traditional field of play is L-shaped (see diagram), with five shallow holes spaced anywhere from 20 to 45 feet apart. The dimensions can be modified to fit available space and the age and ability of the players. The holes are fairly shallow, so that the marbles come to rest in them rather than rolling into them.

Tahlequah, Oklahoma, the capital of the Cherokee Nation, hosts an annual Cherokee Marbles tournament. Many signs in Tahlequah appear in the Cherokee language, the phonetic pronunciation of the Cherokee, and English.

45

○ The game starts at the second hole, where each player throws a marble back to the first hole to determine who goes first (first one to land in the hole).

○ All the players from each team take turns and must land their marbles in all five holes in sequence. Once a player lands in the second hole, he or she can start to hit opponent's marbles out of the way.

○ After landing in the fifth hole, players must roll their marbles back to the first four holes in succession before a winner is declared.

○ Marbles must be rolled from the spot where they land; throwing them is not permitted.

○ A player may only hit another player's marble twice before making the next hole. Hitting an opponent's marble earns an additional throw, which can be directed at another marble or at a hole.

Strategy. Hitting an opponent's marble on purpose allows you to go again, but hitting another's marble by mistake calls for a missed turn, which means much of the game relies on the honor system. Tournaments have judges, but casual games develop great skills of conflict resolution the old-fashioned way — by agreeing to disagree.

ROUND ROCKS

From the time the game began around 800 CE until recent years, tribes played it with the roundest rocks they could find. Making the marbles, in fact, required more skill than playing the game. Often they were chipped from larger stones into the relatively uniform size of the modern billiard ball and carefully polished to bring out the natural beauty of the stone. Masters such as Dennis Sixkiller still hone marbles this time-honored way.

CHINESE JUMP ROPE

ALSO KNOWN AS
Chinese Garters,
Elastics, French
Skipping, German
Jumping, Gummitwist,
Jumpsies, Mississippi,
Rubber Twist, Skip
Tape, Yoki

Instead of a rope spinning through the air, the game of Chinese jump rope utilizes a long rope tied in a loop or a large elastic band in an activity that resembles the hand game of cat's cradle. Mentioned in Chinese literature at least 1,600 years ago, Chinese jump rope was hugely popular on American playgrounds from the 1950s through the 1980s, but seems to have lost favor with the reduction of recess at many schools.

Hop to It

Although the moves can be complex, the core game couldn't be simpler. Two players, called "holders" or "enders," usually begin by wrapping a looped rope or series of elastic bands around their ankles to form parallel lines. A jumper hops in and out of the ropes in a series of patterns, which are called out by the enders, often in a rhythm or song.

If the jumper fails to execute the pattern, one of the enders becomes the jumper and the game continues for as long as the three players agree the game is fun. It's wonderful training for all sorts of other sports, games, and dances, and a great way for children to exercise without even realizing it.

Rules. The rope and how it is held is the initial key to Chinese jump rope. The idea is to hold it taut but not rigid, so players don't trip and fall. Games can also be improvised with elastic bands, wide ribbons, or pantyhose woven together in a loop with a circumference of 10 feet or longer.

○ Play usually advances so that the rope is crisscrossed to make the jump patterns more complicated.

○ The height of the rope is also adjusted upward — from ankles, to knees, to waist or even chest high — to increase the challenge, especially for older players.

Calling out the movements, or patterns, is where much of the camaraderie is revealed. Commands can be as easy as "in" or "out" or far more advanced. In "Mississippi," for example, the enders call out the letters of the 20th state, with each letter corresponding to a specific move:

M	Jump to the center
I	Move both feet outside the ropes
S	Jump to the left, one foot inside
S	Jump to the right, opposite foot inside
I	Move both feet outside the ropes
S	Jump to the left, one foot inside
S	Jump to the right, opposite foot inside
I	Move both feet outside the ropes
PP	Land with both feet on top of the ropes
I	Start over or let a new jumper begin

49

Chinese jump rope, a kinder, gentler version of Double Dutch (see page 76), is enjoyed by children around the world, including Turkey, as shown here.

Variation: Jump the Shot

This Swedish game, which is at least several hundred years old, is still featured in some Boy Scout manuals. It is played with one person holding the end of the rope at the center of a circle. All the players in the circle must jump over the spinning rope without getting hit and the last player standing wins. Long ago, a bag of buckshot or gunpowder was tied to the free end of the rope to keep it taut, hence the name. These days, a beanbag replaces the buckshot.

Anthony "Buddy" Lee, an All-American wrestler at Old Dominion University who competed in the 1992 Barcelona Summer Olympics, founded the Jump Rope Institute in 1996. The organization promotes all forms of jump roping, including Chinese jump rope.

Cave Jumpers

Jumping rope as a human activity is most likely tens of thousands of years old, but no one seems to know for sure. A book titled *The History and Science of Knots* noted that the first clear evidence of human-made rope was discovered in the caves at Lascaux in southern France, which date to 15,000 BCE. Cave drawings dating to 5000 BCE seem to depict children jumping rope.

50

It would be impossible to imagine a young child of any culture not being tempted to toss an object — whether it be a rock, a bone, or a ball — into a simple hole. Native American cultures describe all types of tossing games in their early writings and in oral histories passed down through generations. Germans in the 1400s were known to play a version of beanbag toss, a game that is described in several North American books of games from the early twentieth century.

THE SETUP

BASIC IDEA
Take turns tossing
beanbags at the target;
closest one scores

PLAYING AREA
Any grassy or
paved area

EQUIPMENT
• 2 slanted boards with
  a hole near one end
• 4 bean bags per team
  (bags can also be
  filled with dry corn)

AGES
3 and up

PLAYERS
2 to 4

Bonkers for Beanbags

Cornhole, played using a rectangular board
measuring approximately two feet wide and
four feet long, emerged as the primary name
of the game in the past 20 years or so in either
Cincinnati, Ohio, or Chicago, Illinois, depending
on whose story you believe. As vague as the
origins of the name might be, one thing is
certain: Everything changed when marketing
guru Frank Geers began playing.

"I've played cornhole in every corner of
this great cornholing country of ours," says
the Cincinnati-based founder of the American

Premade cornhole sets are readily available or you can make your
own (look for plans online).

Cornhole Organization (ACO). "I've pitched cornhole bags from the Queen City to Sin City. America needs the next great family game and this is it."

Although Geers said his favorite cornhole matches are the spontaneous ones he enjoys with his three sons in his own backyard, he has helped move the game from the west side of Cincinnati to the parking lot of Cincinnati Bengals games and into the mainstream. Cornhole boards can now be purchased bearing the logos of all the other National Football League and many college teams, as well as many other corporate logos. Tournaments sanctioned by Geers' ACO offer prize money in the tens of thousands of dollars.

Film director Timothy Clarke made a feature film called Cornhole: The Movie, *a "mockumentary" about four fictitious cornhole fanatics who make their way to one of the alleged birthplaces of the sport, Cincinnati, Ohio. The film premiered to a packed audience of real cornhole aficionados at the Madison Theater in Covington, Kentucky, on May 7, 2010.*

53

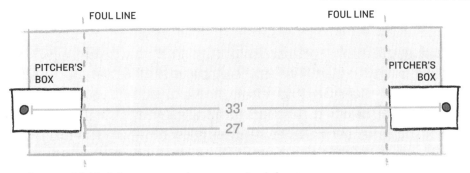

FOUL LINE   FOUL LINE

PITCHER'S BOX   PITCHER'S BOX

33'
27'

Suggested field of play; younger players may stand closer

Rules. Scored like horseshoes and quoits, with games to 21, cornhole requires players to earn points by landing their bags (filled with beans or corn or some synthetic material) somewhere on the surface of the board. Cancellation scoring is usually used, meaning that the team with the most points per inning subtracts the other team's total, leaving a net total. That prevents the games from ending too quickly.

○ **Two opposing players stand by each board and toss at the farther board; individual players aim at a single board.**

○ **Each player tosses four bags per inning, with the pair of opponents at one end pitching all the bags before the other pair plays.**

○ **A bag in the hole is worth three points; landing on the board is worth one.**

○ **Knocking an opponent's bag off the board is permitted.**

○ **A bag that hits the ground before landing on the board is considered a foul and is removed from the board. If the foul knocks another bag off the board, that bag is replaced.**

Strategy. Because bags often stop just short of the hole, strategy always comes into play. If an opponent's bag is blocking the hole, for example, you might use a high arching toss to try to land your bag directly in the hole so that it doesn't inadvertently knock in the opponent's bag for three points. Some players prefer a low, fast toss that slides toward the hole from the base of the board, which is angled at about 20 degrees.

Rules govern the distance from the board for official matches, but for family games in the backyard, the throwing line can be set up at any distance.

" LEARN THE LINGO "

Ace A bag that lands on the board

Air mail A bag that goes straight into a hole

Dirty bag A bag that misses the board entirely

Hanger A bag that dangles on the edge of a hole — worth two points

Sally A bag that lands well short of the board

Shucker A bag that knocks another bag off the board

"Cornfusion," as you might guess, arises when players can't agree on the proper scoring totals.

UPPING THE ANTE

Some versions of bean-bag toss have multiple holes on the boards, which can be square or round, with varying point totals assigned to each hole (see Chinese horseshoes, page 115). The highest point total is usually reserved for the highest hole on the board.

These games were derived from a popular arcade game, skeeball, which was invented in 1907 by Joseph Fourestier Simpson of Vineland, New Jersey, and later improved by Princeton graduate Jonathan Dickinson Este.

55

CRAB SOCCER

ALSO KNOWN AS
Cage Ball,
Crab Football

As the world's most popular sport, soccer can and should be enjoyed by players of all ages. Many children learn to kick before they can throw and, given the tender physiology of growing bodies, it's far safer for young children to play kicking games than throwing games. The basic game of soccer needs no further introduction. Here, we present a first cousin known as "crab soccer," which is just about the most fun game you can play on all fours.

THE SETUP

BASIC IDEA
Score goals while
moving like a crab

PLAYING AREA
A smooth, soft lawn

EQUIPMENT
• A ball
• Markers for
  boundaries and goal

AGES
5 and up

PLAYERS
At least 3 on 3

Start Scuttling

Crab soccer can be contested with a standard soccer ball, but it's meant to be played with a giant cage ball up to 6 feet in diameter. The bigger the ball, the better, because more team-work is required to advance the ball forward. The game gets its name from the position of the players, who scuttle around on feet and hands, bellies up, in "crab walk" fashion. It's fantastic exercise that teaches agility and builds core strength, but mostly it just makes kids laugh!

57

Rules. Because the game is inherently tiring, the field size is generally laid out in proportion to how many players are available on each side. Some gym classes will pit 20 against 20, but in a backyard setting of 3 against 3, a 30-foot-long field is plenty big.

- The goal of the game is identical to that of regular soccer: to score goals.

- Field players cannot hit the ball with their hands or cradle the ball on their stomachs.

- The only player allowed to stand or touch the ball with his or her hands is the goalie.

- Players at rest can sit on the ground, but any movement toward the ball must be belly up on all fours.

- Many rules require that one foot be on the ground while a player is in the act of kicking, so that the overly powerful "roll" or "cycle" kicks are not allowed.

- Other rules require that the ball always remain low to the ground.

- Kicking and pushing other players is never allowed.

In some versions of the game, especially if adults are concerned about opposing teams of crab soccer players harming each other, play is against the clock and a single goalie. The ball must be touched by all players as it is advanced down the field toward the goal; in three to five minutes, the team tries to score as many goals as possible before the other team takes its turn.

Variation: Omnikin

The game of Omnikin, or Kin–Ball, uses the same giant cage ball adapted for crab soccer. In this game, the players from a minimum of three teams are standing. One team, in which all players must be touching the ball, hollers out the color or name of one of the other teams and hits the ball into the air. That team must keep the ball from hitting the floor for 10 seconds before advancing it to one of the other teams. Players are not allowed to catch or cradle the ball. If a team fails to keep the ball aloft for 10 seconds, the other team is awarded points.

«FLASHBACK VICTORIA«

They really should call this game "giggle ball" because it guarantees gales of laughter, whether the players are 6 or 46 years old, and it's a great workout, too. Try crab racing against your kids and see who can hold up the longest. Go for personal-best records, maneuver around an obstacle course, balance a toy on your tummy while you scuttle — it's a guaranteed good time!

NO HUSTLING ALLOWED

Variations of soccer have been played around the world for at least 3,000 years. On April 13, 1314, King Edward II decreed that "this hustling over large balls" must be banned because of the negative impact on the lives of merchants in cities and towns.

59

CROQUET

ALSO KNOWN AS
Gateball, Malletball,
Pall Mall, Roque

Although it was contested as an Olympic sport in France in 1900 and serious matches are played the world over today, croquet ranks with bocce as a quintessential family lawn game. This game, combining skill and strategy with camaraderie and laughter, deserves a fresh look and a permanent space in the sheds, garages, and game closets of the future.

THE SETUP

BASIC IDEA
Hit the ball with
the mallet through
the hoops in a
certain order

PLAYING AREA
Backyard croquet
can be played on any
turf mowed to about
3 inches. A few undu-
lations and bumps add
a little extra challenge.

EQUIPMENT
• 6 balls
• 6 mallets
• 9 metal wickets
• 2 stakes

AGES
5 and up

PLAYERS
2 to 6, individually or
in teams

Start 'em Young

Give a toddler a ball and chances are he or she will immediately throw, kick, or bounce it. Soon after, on the developmental continuum, the child will whack the ball with a stick — or in this case, a mallet. Because the ball isn't moving as it does in many games, croquet is one of the best games to teach hand–eye coordination. By age 3, many children can at least grasp the concept of tapping the ball through a hoop. Within a few years, children can be earnest participants in croquet games with their parents, grandparents, and even great-grandparents. How many other games can truly offer a seven- or eight-decade spread in the ages of the players?

Rules. Several official versions of the game exist, using either six wickets or nine, two to six players, and prescribed field sizes up to 100 feet long and 50 feet wide. Backyard games, however, can be set up on a patch of lawn large or small and any manner of house rules can be adopted.

61

- Players hit their balls through the wickets or hoops in a preordained succession.

- Balls can be hit off other balls, much like billiards, and therein lies much of the strategy.

- The first player to advance the ball through all the wickets and hit a stake at the end of the course is the winner.

Strategy. Risk versus reward is a major consideration in the strategy of this game, as is vengeance. How forcefully, for example, do you hit your ball toward the wicket? If you hit the ball too hard and it misses, it can roll past the wicket and necessitate a makeup or backward shot on your next turn. If you leave your ball right in front of a wicket, but don't get it through, the next players in line may easily hit it out of position.

Hitting another player's ball, known as "roqueting," gives you a two-stroke bonus. You can use both of these strokes to advance your own ball, or use one of them to send an opponent's ball off course. This is done by positioning your ball right next to the ball just hit, then placing your foot firmly on top of your ball. When you whack your ball (be careful not to whack your ankle!), it won't move, but your opponent's will. Mastering this technique is essential to fully enjoying croquet's cutthroat nature!

" LEARN THE LINGO "

Peg out To cause a rover ball to hit the last stake, ending its participation in the game

Roquet To hit another player's ball with your own

Rover ball In team play, a ball that has gone through all the wickets but remains in play to help teammates

Send To move another player's ball off course

Tice A ball that has landed in a location that will entice an opponent to shoot at it, but most likely miss

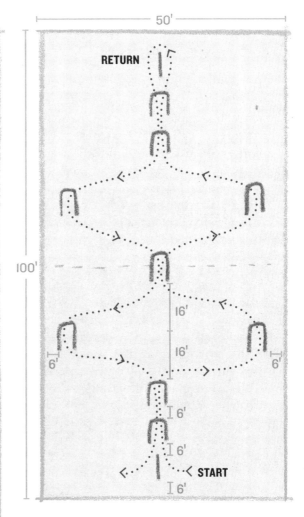

This is the official setup for a croquet game, but you can set up your wickets in any pattern you desire.

Dotted line indicates the official path of play.

63

Extreme Croquet

Leaving the genteel confines of a well-manicured lawn behind, the game of extreme croquet knows no boundaries — the more hills, tree roots, or even cliffs, the better. "We started playing in the backyard, putting wickets in weird places and then decided it was too small, so we went out to one of the parks. It just went farther and farther," says Bob Warseck, who cofounded the Connecticut Extreme Croquet Society in 1984.

Because the standard equipment breaks easily when whacked against tree roots and rocks, the extreme mallets are fashioned from hardwoods such as ash and birch. Mallet heads are wedge shaped so balls can easily be lifted into the air. Wickets are placed anywhere and everywhere and matches can be daylong outings, complete with picnic baskets and beverages of choice.

The first croquet club in the United States was formed at Newport, Rhode Island, in 1865, and by 1882, a group of 25 clubs formed the National American Croquet Association. Today, the organization sanctions hundreds of tournaments each year and retains an affiliation with the World Croquet Federation's World Championship.

STILL IN BUSINESS

Six million people from around the world visited the first Great Exhibition of the Works of Industry of all Nations, opened by Queen Victoria on May 1, 1851. Among the exhibits were balls and mallets for croquet, manufactured by John Jaques II, who claimed to be the inventor of the game that soon swept across Great Britain.

Because variations of croquet's predecessor, pall mall, have been played since at least the 1400s, his claim may be dubious; however, Jaques of London, founded in 1795, remains the world's oldest commercial manufacturer of children's games.

The French version of this game, paille-maille, was very popular in the time of King James I of England. His grandson, Charles II, played it so often in St James's Park, London, that a nearby road, popular for walking, became known as Pall Mall. A "mall" came to mean an urban area pleasant for walking, and now the meaning extends to shopping malls around the world.

65

DODGEBALL

A facetious historian might place dodgeball at the top of the list as the oldest game on the planet. Presumably, cavemen would have had no qualms about picking up a rock and whipping it toward another caveman who possessed coveted food, shelter, or companionship. That dubious perception may be why certain people consider this game practically barbaric, as if launching a ball at another human being for the sake of pleasure has no place on the playground. In fact, in many communities, dodgeball is banned.

THE SETUP

BASIC IDEA
Be the first team to
eliminate all the
opposing players by
hitting them with a
rubber ball

PLAYING AREA
A smooth, open area
(paved or grassy) with
boundaries to keep the
ball from rolling off

EQUIPMENT
• 5 to 10 balls
• Boundary markers

AGES
5 and up

PLAYERS
At least 3 on 3

"Dodgeball is just not a game that has values that we should be teaching to our children," said Neil Williams, a professor from Eastern Connecticut State College who has been the unofficial leader of a crusade to rid playgrounds of the game.

We're here to say, loudly, clearly, and respectfully, that dodgeball, like British bulldogs (page 33), Red Rover (page 158), and tug of war (page 176), deserves a continued place among the cherished games of the past and future. Absolutely, use the right kind of ball and realize that games may need to be overseen by an adult. Bullying, which is certainly possible in this and so many other children's games, should never be tolerated.

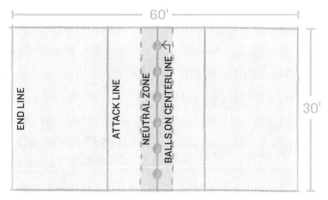

Initial setup

" LEARN THE LINGO "

One of the mistakes inexperienced players make is to throw balls aimlessly. Here are a few key phrases to help you improve your percentage of hits.

The shinsplinter A low ball that is more difficult to catch

The look-away
Looking at one player, but throwing it at another to catch them off guard

The boomerang
Throwing the ball at an opposing player who has just wound up to throw and is momentarily defenseless

Benefits of the Game

With common sense and some restrictions, dodgeball can teach all sorts of beneficial skills, from throwing and catching, spinning, twisting, and balance to tactical consideration of risk/reward strategies — or what military and sports leaders refer to as "situational awareness." In other words, do you stand near the front of the line where the action is, or hang back and wait for your opening?

Rules. Dodgeball is usually played with two to six large rubber balls, the kind used in kickball, inflated to a low pressure of about 1.5 pounds per square inch. Foam-core balls with a soft rubber coating can also be used. Thrown from a reasonable distance (many rules call for at least a 10- or 20-foot minimum) by players of similar age and size, the ball should not inflict bodily harm.

The field is usually broken into equal halves.

○ **Games usually begin with all the balls on the centerline, though they can also be evenly divided between the teams.**

○ Players line up along the end lines and sprint toward the balls to gather as many as possible for an opening advantage. They may roll the balls back to their teammates but may not begin throwing at opponents until back out of the neutral zone.

○ The goal is for one team to eliminate all the players on the other team. A player is "out" if:
  • He or she is hit by a thrown ball from the shoulders down
  • A player on the other team catches a ball thrown by the player before the ball hits the ground
  • A ball bounces off a teammate and hits the player
  • The player steps out of bounds

○ Players can re-enter a game either by catching a thrown ball while standing on the sidelines or by getting called back in by a teammate who has just caught a ball inside the court.

Strategy. A key strategy is for multiple teammates, each with a ball, to pick one player to throw the ball at; it's difficult to dodge or catch more than one ball at a time. It's that gang-up strategy, of course, that gives the game its negative reputation in some circles; however, given safe balls and a proper distance, it's all in good fun.

Variation: Spud

In this simplified American version of dodgeball, one player tosses the ball straight up into the air and calls out another player's name. While the ball tosser and other players scatter, the named player must retrieve the ball and holler "Spud!" The running players must instantly freeze in place.

The "it" player then throws the ball at another player; if the ball hits the player, he or she gets an "S"; however, if the player catches the ball, the thrower receives the "S." The last player to reach S-P-U-D is the

Clearly, teachers in the 1930s were less concerned with playground safety than they are today. At least the windows are open, reducing the chance of broken glass.

winner. Defending players are not allowed to move their feet, but can contort their bodies to avoid getting hit.

In a variation that is considered safer in some circles, the "it" player must roll the ball at the other players' feet. That eliminates the risk of bruises or bruised egos, especially if the sizes and ability of players vary.

Variation: Ga-ga

A playground version of dodgeball from Israel is played inside a circle of people or within an octagonal court made especially for the game. Homemade courts can easily be constructed with fences, benches, woodpiles, sheets of plywood, or picnic tables turned on their sides.

The ball is batted off the wall or toward other players with an open hand or closed fist and a player hit by the ball at or below the knees is eliminated. In this game, though, a player may simply bat the ball in a new direction with his or her hands and many of the "hits" happen on caroms off the wall. No player can hit the ball twice in a row, unless only two players remain. This can be played as a team game, but usually it's an all-for-one free-for-all!

HISTORICALLY SPEAKING

We couldn't find dodgeball in any references of children's activities in the 1800s, but author Emmett Dunn Angell did include the game in his landmark book, *Play: Comprising Games for the Kindergarten, Playground, Schoolroom and College*, published in 1910.

Angell described a dodgeball game played in a circle, with a single stiff leather basketball. One team's players played within the circle, trying to dodge throws from the players who were forming the human ring.

DOUBLE BALL

Deeply spiritual to Native Americans, the game of double ball combined elements of their ancient sport of lacrosse with Ultimate Frisbee and ladder golf centuries before the latter two activities even existed. Played with a double ball or bolas (see ladder toss, page 133), which was propelled by players carrying thin tree branches, the ancient game was contested across miles-long playing fields. The games, which sometimes served as dispute settlements among tribes, could last for entire days. In some tribes, only the women played double ball; the men played lacrosse.

THE SETUP

BASIC IDEA
Teammates toss the bolas back and forth while running to score goals

PLAYING AREA
The more players, the larger the area

EQUIPMENT
• One double ball
• A stick for each player
• Safety goggles might be a good idea

AGES
10 and up

PLAYERS
4 or more per team

Play Bolas

Nowadays, games are typically limited to soccer- and football-sized fields, or even smaller areas, especially if younger children and fewer players are involved. Long games require great stamina, coordination, and athleticism, but probably the best aspect of the game is the charm of the equipment: no two balls or sticks are alike.

Double balls were traditionally made by filling two pouches of deerskin with buffalo hair and joining them with a foot-long leather thong or tethering two dowels together with rawhide. Modern variations of the ball are often made from a couple of beanbags tied together.

Homemade double balls can be crafted by putting sand or small pebbles in the end of a tube sock or legging and tying it off so that the sand stays balled up in the bottom, then adding an equal amount of sand or stones in the remaining space, and sealing up the open end of the sock. Tie off above the second ball, creating a short "bridge" of sock fabric between the two sacks.

Rules. Teams score single points by throwing the double ball between, over, or under the football-style goal posts at each end of the field.

- The game begins when a referee or a player throws the ball high into the air at the center of the field.

- Players from both sides run toward the ball and try to catch it on their stick.

- Most rules allow the ball to be advanced only by throwing and catching, but some variations allow running with the ball until a player passes or shoots, or it's knocked off the stick by an opponent.

- When the ball touches the ground, it can either be picked up by the opposing team or thrown into the air at the drop spot by the referee.

- Three points are awarded if the ball wraps around the crossbar of the goal posts, two if the ball flies over the crossbar, and one if it flies under the bar.

Strategy. In some games, points are deleted from a team's total if the ball is allowed to drop to the ground. That places a high premium on learning to catch and throw the ball with the stick, which is usually about three feet long.

Although young players will inevitably have the urge to cluster toward the ball, the most successful teams learn to spread the field with equal numbers of offensive and defensive players. That ensures a place in the game for the fastest and slowest runners, and everyone in between.

World Champs

The young Native American women of the Fort Shaw Government Indian Boarding School became an international phenomenon at the 1904 St. Louis World's Fair in conjunction with that year's Olympics.

Taking on all comers in the new American sport of basketball, the women from various Plains tribes reportedly won every contest and received a trophy that declared them to be World's Fair champions. The women's remarkable endurance on the court was attributed to having played double ball as children, according to the 2008 book, *Full Court Quest*.

The Native Wellness Institute, one of the nation's leading non-profit organizations dedicated to preserving Native American wellness-related training, still teaches double ball to children within tribes across North America. Their games always begin with a ceremony and prayer.

"We must give thanks to the Creator for what he has given us, and I don't mean TVs and cell phones. I'm talking about the gift of motion," said Charlie Tailfeathers, Sr., a founding member of the Institute, formed in 2000 in Gresham, Oregon.

DOUBLE DUTCH

Give a young child an object, any object, and he or she will make a game or a toy out of it. Give a child a rope and the possibilities are almost endless, from jumping to tying and lassoing. But if you give three children two ropes, well, look out! The amazement was reportedly palpable on the streets of a trading town on the Hudson River known as New Amsterdam more than 300 years ago. When new British settlers saw two young Dutch children simultaneously twirling two ropes in opposite directions, with other children

THE SETUP

BASIC IDEA
Perform a variety
of jumps, spins, and
gymnastics while
negotiating 2
spinning ropes

PLAYING AREA
Any lawn, paved
area, indoor gym, or
dance floor

EQUIPMENT
2 pieces of rope
at least 10 feet
(3 m) long

AGES
Starting around 8,
although some prodi-
gies are younger

PLAYERS
A minimum of 3, can
be as many as 30

jumping in the middle, the game of Double Dutch began to take hold in what we now call New York City.

Jump to It

Perhaps the game that requires the most endurance and athletic ability of any in this book, Double Dutch involves a rare combination of coordination, timing, and rhythm. A syncopated form of the simple game of jump rope, Double Dutch is at least four times as difficult, but maybe 10 times the fun once you have it mastered.

Double Dutch offers the joy of music as well as movement, since singing and rhyming is most often conducted as an accompaniment. The game also fuses friendships and/or fans competitive fires, because you must carefully study the best rope swingers and jumpers. One false move by anyone can throw an entire team off its game.

Rules. The official records are kept based on making a certain number of jumps in a set period of time and, believe it or not, the world's best teams can make up to six jumps in a

77

second. "Fusion" teams combine acrobatics and dance with jumping, and judges' scores, along with the number of jumps, determine who wins. For the basics, simply choose two players to twirl the ropes and at least one person to jump in.

- Left arms turn the rope clockwise and right arms turn the rope counterclockwise. Hold the rope between your thumb and index finger and twirl from the elbow until you gain experience.

- Finding a rhythm is important; that's why having all players sing the same song helps.

78

DOUBLE PHOENICIAN?

Historians trace the likely origin of Double Dutch to ancient Chinese, Phoenician, and Egyptian rope makers. With strands of hemp around their waists attached to a spinning wheel, the workers moved backward, twisting the material uniformly as they walked. Other workers in the buildings or on the docks had to jump over the rope as it formed to avoid tripping or becoming entangled. This was before the days of workers' compensation!

" LEARN THE LINGO "

Eggbeater The act of spinning the ropes in opposite directions simultaneously

Freestyle The act of spontaneously improvising new jumps within the ropes

SSJ "Super speed jumper," the name given to individuals who try to see how many jumps they can make in two minutes

The South Carolina team of Antoine Cutner, Ernest Gilmore, Joy Hiller, and Cita Wise set the all-time team speed record in Double Dutch in 2005 with an astonishing 879 jumps in 2 minutes.

79

«FLASHBACK VICTORIA«

As a farm girl from Maine, it was very, very important that I learned how to play Double Dutch when I moved to Boston in fifth grade, because it was such a part of the culture in my new urban neighborhood. Having had some ballet lessons, I was into rhythm and at least had some potential, but this is not an easy game to master. I worked hard at it.

It was really something to go to the playground and see all those ropes twirling in rhythm. My heart would begin beating fast just in the anticipation of participating! Some of the girls were more polished than others and I was lucky that the ones I was playing with were very encouraging. I'll never forget the moment I "got it" and enjoyed my first time inside the ropes and being the center of everyone's attention! I had such a sense of achievement; I had been accepted.

FIELD HOCKEY

ALSO KNOWN AS
Bandy, Camogie,
Hurling, Lawn
Hockey, Shinny

One of the most popular sports around the world, field hockey has been contested for at least 4,000 years, yet remains under-appreciated in the United States, where ice hockey enjoys a vastly higher social standing. A goal-scoring game, field hockey was described compellingly in a 1903 Spalding sports manual meant to introduce the game to the American masses: "The vigorous running gives splendid development of heart and lung power, even surpassing football in this respect. The player gets the wrist of a fencer and the

THE SETUP

BASIC IDEA
Players with sticks pass the ball along the ground while trying to score goals

PLAYING AREA
A fairly large field with smooth grass

EQUIPMENT
- A hard rubber ball (a tennis ball works in a pinch)
- A stick for each player (preferably field hockey sticks, but ice hockey ones will do)
- Markers for boundaries
- 2 goals

AGES
5 and up

PLAYERS
2 on 2, up to 11 on 11

accuracy of a golfer, for he must be able to twist the ball quickly from his opponent and pick it up and dribble it along at his greatest speed down the field . . . "

Not Just for Girls

Male Americans might not have bought into that argument, but it's never too late to join the tens of millions of women, and men from other nations, who appreciate the game's nuances. Informal field hockey games played on any backyard or playground, with any manner of equipment, can be a great cardiovascular work-out and develop hand-eye coordination.

Rules. In terms of field size and player count, field hockey is quite similar to soccer, with a 100-yard field and 11 players on a side. The game's slender stick — about three feet long and curved at the bottom — gives the game its primary distinction. At the curve, the stick is flat on one side and rounded on the other; only the flat side may be used to strike the ball.

81

○ Teams comprise forwards (or "inners"), midfielders, and backers, and the simple objective is to outscore the other team.

○ Play begins with all players in position and the ball placed between the two center forwards, who battle for initial possession.

○ Players may dribble or pass the ball toward the opposing goal, but the ball must remain below knee level. Sticks may not be raised above the shoulder on the backswing.

○ Players are not permitted to kick the ball and only two players at a time may be touching the ball with their sticks.

○ Shots on goal must come from within the circle, unless an offensive player is completely unguarded from outside the arch.

Strategy. The best players spend hours upon hours mastering their stick technique. Controlling the ball by dribbling, pushing, flicking, scooping, hitting, and driving is essential as teammates move toward the opponent's goal.

Olympic MVP

Few sports are unanimous in the selection of greatest player of all time, but in field hockey the overwhelming choice is Dhyan Chand, a captain in the Indian Army. He was the leading goal scorer for three consecutive Olympic titles: Amsterdam in 1928, Los Angeles in 1932, and Berlin in 1936. India still celebrates Chand's birthday, August 29, as National Sports Day.

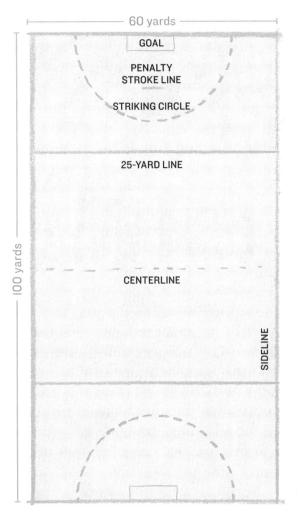

The advent of AstroTurf in the mid-1960s impacted all sports, but none more than field hockey, where the ball is played almost entirely on the ground. This "synthetic revolution" ended the dominance of India and Pakistan in world competition because those countries initially could not afford fake grass fields. Equipment, techniques, and rules changed to accommodate the increased speed of the game, which now requires artificial turf in all major tournaments.

Official layout for field hockey; a backyard game can be any size that is available or suited to the number of players.

FLAG FOOTBALL

Although the international game of football, which Americans call soccer, has been played the world over for millennia, the U.S. version has been around for only about a century. And while most of us are too small, slow, frail, or otherwise ill-equipped to play the helmet-crashing version, just about everyone can enjoy a game of touch or flag football in the backyard.

Although the game evolved from a time when the emphasis was on kicking and running, it's the forward pass, which wasn't even

THE SETUP

BASIC IDEA
Run or pass the ball up the field to score a touchdown without being "deflagged"

PLAYING AREA
A large, open area

EQUIPMENT
• A football
• A flag for each player (optional); flags can be bandanas stuck in back pockets or fabric strips attached by Velcro to a belt

AGES
8 and up

PLAYERS
2 on 2, up to 11 on 11

legal in the game's official rules until 1906, that makes football such challenging, thrilling fun. Children beam with pride when they learn to catch the ball or throw their first touchdown pass. The male youth of North America often grow up dreaming of being the next iconic quarterback — a Unitas, Namath, or Brady — however remote the chances may be.

Down, Set, Hut!

The fundamental point of football is to advance the ball, by running with it or passing it to a teammate, down the field past the goal line and into the end zone. The "real" game's myriad rules and nuances can take years to fully comprehend and grown men who have been around the game their entire lives still debate rules every Sunday. Numerous flag football leagues, likewise, have a plethora of regulations, but in the backyard, house rules are invariably more informal.

The primary difference is that in flag football much of the roughhousing is removed. The game is terrific not only for developing skills and athleticism, but also for rewarding

85

NO NEANDERTHAL FOOTBALL

For millions of years, the ability to throw rocks, spears, and darts has given humankind its edge at the top of the food chain. A lack of throwing ability, according to archeologists, is what led Neanderthals to their extinction.

Although American football probably evolved from British rugby (well after the Neanderthal era), a similar game, called *cuju* or "kickball," has been played in China for at least 2,000 years, complete with goal posts and a feather-stuffed ball. The first air-filled ball, a blown-up animal bladder, came into existence around 600 CE.

teamwork, strategy, and conflict resolution. Regardless of the outcome of a pass or run, players always regroup in a huddle to design the next play. What a thrill indeed when everything works out as planned — with the ball in the end zone!

Rules. Some basics are always the same. Two goal lines are marked parallel and opposite from each other. The official distance is 100 yards, but the game can be played on any patch of grass or sand that seems reasonable for the number of players, usually no more than 11 against 11.

- **In pickup games, teams are usually given four tries or "downs" to advance the ball from their end zone down the length of the field.**

- **Teams might agree not to kick off at the beginning of the game or after a touchdown, but rather to begin the play at a given spot on the field.**

- Rather than tackling a player who is passing, or running with the ball, opponents either touch the player with one or both hands, or try to grab a flag that is loosely attached to every player's waist.

- Quarterbacks are usually afforded time to throw the ball before being chased by an opponent, who must give a count of about four seconds before dashing in pursuit.

Touch football has been played since at least the 1920s, but adding flags to the game first gained widespread acceptance at Fort Meade in Odenton, Maryland, during World War II. By then, football had become the nation's most popular pickup sport among young men, but injuries suffered during rough versions of "touch" put too many soldiers into the infirmary. Flag football was first mentioned in Webster's Dictionary in 1954.

«FLASHBACK PAUL«

As much as I enjoy playing outdoor games of all sorts, I have to say that football is my all-time favorite and that that has everything to do with the ball itself. Evolved from the first rugby balls made in London in the early 1800s — based on the oval shape of a pig's bladder — the football is unlike any other ball in existence. It isn't a natural object to bounce, kick, catch, or especially throw, but once you master it, tossing the ball back and forth can become a lifelong addiction.

And because the ball is larger and heavier (but not too heavy) than other sport balls, it's actually easier on the arm and shoulder than throwing, say, a baseball, which causes the rotator cuff to open and close at a higher rate of speed. Far more children develop sore arms from tossing baseballs than footballs.

Although purists typically feel that a true football game must be played with a leather ball, the Parker Brothers company revolutionized youth games in 1970 with the introduction of balls made from nonexpanding recreational foam, better known as NERF balls. The 1972 introduction of the wildly popular NERF football allowed the tossing of a ball indoors and gave legions of would-be quarterbacks their first experience at throwing a spiral pass.

88

FLYING DISC

Perhaps the only truly modern invention showcased in this book, the flying disc trademarked and commonly known as the "Frisbee" may well be the single outdoor game creation of the twentieth century that will still be played many millennia from now. The aerodynamic molded plastic toy, for which there is no precedent other than maybe the pie tin, has provided modern children and adults — and dogs — with a whole range of athletic activities that are enjoyed the world over.

THE SETUP

BASIC IDEA
Toss the disc from one player to another; add rules as desired

PLAYING AREA
A large, flat area is best and safest, although discs can be thrown great distances over hilly terrain.

EQUIPMENT
- A flying disc
- Targets (for Frisbee golf)
- Posts or shovels (for Ding)

AGES
5 and up

PLAYERS
2 or more

Frisbees can be incorporated into almost any type of outdoor game. Target Frisbee, Frisbee golf, and Ding reward excellent skill in throwing the grooved disc. Ultimate and discathon require high levels of speed and endurance. In the end, though, this is a toy that can be enjoyed by players of all ages in a simple game of catch in the backyard. Properly clad folks in the Victorian era would have loved the Frisbee, had they only had one.

Rules & Strategy

The first step for any would-be Frisbee player is to learn the basics of the throw and catch.

- **The simple toss requires a backhand flick of the wrist with your thumb on top of the disc and the other four fingers balancing it underneath.**

- **Keeping the disc level on release helps ensure a straight throw; angling the disc will cause it to curve in one direction or the other.**

- Torque your arms, shoulders, hips, and legs in unison with your hands and wrist to throw the disc great distances.

Several techniques can be used to catch the aerodynamic plastic.

- Beginners can grab the flying disc by clapping it between their hands as it approaches — it's all in the timing!

- More advanced players learn to pluck the disc with a one-hand clutch of the spinning edge.

- Frisbee wizards can stop the flight with a single index finger on the underside of the disc, which spins to a halt after several revolutions.

Once the basic toss and catch are mastered, the rules can be what you make them. The formal games, from Frisbee golf to Ultimate, have official rules available from national and international associations; however, nothing more than the Frisbee itself is needed for a full day of fun. Players can range in age from 5 to 85. Targets can be trees and posts.

WHAT'S IN A NAME?

A baker named William Russell Frisbie, who ran a shop in Bridgeport, Connecticut, stamped his name in the bottom of his pie tins. Students at nearby Yale University took to tossing the metal tins though the air, hollering out "Frisbie" as they threw. Talk about a good marketing scheme!

In 1958, the same year that the Wham-O company's Hula Hoop exploded onto the American market (see page 108), the company borrowed the baker's name, trademarked as Frisbee, and changed the original name of its flying disc from "Pluto Platter." Sales exploded, with an estimated 250 million purchased in the past 50 years.

91

Variations

DING

In the game of Ding, four shovels or other posts are stuck in the ground, two on each end of the lawn, with the handles two feet apart. These serve as goal posts and a Frisbee thrown between the handles scores two points. Some versions of Ding include paper cups placed upside down on the top of the shovel handles. If a Frisbee hits a shovel and sends a cup flying, a player from the opposite team must catch the cup before it hits the ground; otherwise, a point is scored.

DISC GOLF

As in regular golf, disc golf rewards target-shooting skill. The player or players to hit a series of targets with the disc in the fewest tries is the winner. The Professional Disc Golf Association publishes all kinds of rules that include creating official baskets with chain nets as targets; however, for backyard games, anything can be a target, including trees, swing sets, lamp posts, and mailboxes.

ULTIMATE

Popular on college campuses since its origins in the late 1960s, Ultimate involves teams of seven tossing the disc to one another with the aim of moving it into the other team's end zone. All movement of the disc must be by throwing; players may pivot and turn to make the throw, but must keep one foot planted on the ground. Games can be played to 13, 15, or 17 points.

DISC DOG

Almost from the moment the Frisbee craze caught on, many pet owners found their dogs could catch the discs, too. Disc dog's breakthrough moment, however, came in the middle of the 8th inning of another sport. On August 5, 1974, just before the Los Angeles Dodgers came to bat, 19-year-old Ohio State University student Alex Stein leapt over the wall at Cincinnati's Riverfront Stadium with his dog, Ashley Whippet, at his side and two Frisbees in his hand.

With the crowd, players, and a national television audience watching for eight minutes, the dog became an instant cult hero by making dozens of dazzling twisting, leaping catches up to nine feet off the ground. Stein was arrested and fined $250, but he and Ashley were soon regulars at every major stadium and talk show in the United States, and disc dog soon became an international canine sport.

The current world record disc toss was achieved by Christian Sandstrom of Sweden, who threw a Frisbee 250 meters in 2002 at a contest in El Mirage, California.

93

FOLLOW THE LEADER

ALSO KNOWN AS
Copycat, Simon Says

Whether it involves jumping, clapping, singing, dancing, or just making funny noises, Follow the Leader just may be the most joyous game of our classic collection. A lifetime activity, the game teaches attention skills and expands horizons for children and creates social breakthroughs and bonds for adults; mostly, however, it just seems to make people laugh.

It's all up to the leader. If he or she flails hands wildly, then everyone else in line follows suit. If the leader squeals like a pig, the rest of

BASIC IDEA
Players follow the actions of the designated leader, no matter how silly

PLAYING AREA
A flat surface free of tripping hazards is essential because players will have their eyes focused on the leader rather than the ground.

EQUIPMENT
A blindfold (optional)

AGES
4 and up

PLAYERS
3 or more

the group is obliged to do likewise. When all of this plays out in a wide-open area of a lawn or playground, the possibilities are endless. How about trying Lucy's grape stomp from the 1956 television show, Chubby Checker's twist, or Michael Jackson's moonwalk? Just watching everyone try those moves is a recipe for hilarity.

Make Your Own Rules

The game can be played just for fun or competitive elements can be added. For example, in one version, one player is blindfolded while another is quietly tapped as the leader.

○ Everyone arranges in a circle around the blindfolded player and begins to follow the moves of the leader, trying not to make it clear who is actually leading.

○ After eye contact and a nod to indicate everyone is ready, the players call out "Copycat, copycat, can you see?"

○ The player in the center removes the blindfold and tries to guess the identity of the leader.

○ If he or she is correct, the leader becomes the next guesser. If the guess is wrong, the blindfold goes back on, the group picks a new leader to follow, and the game continues.

Another version is set up as a relay race.

○ The leader stands on one end of the field and the rest of the players divide into two teams, who form single-file lines at the other end.

○ The leader calls out commands such as "hop," "skip," "somersault," or "run," while a player on each team races toward the leader and back to the line to tag the next teammate's hand.

○ The first team to have all of its members complete the relay wins.

One of our favorite variations pairs two-person teams in a race, with one player on each team blindfolded.

○ Without touching the blindfolded player, the leader must guide his or her teammate through an obstacle course using only verbal commands and cues.

FOLLOW CAREFULLY

Children at the Knife River Indian Village in South Dakota, where Sacagawea joined the Lewis and Clark expedition in 1804, played a version of Follow the Leader that translates to "Follow the Bad Road."

According to a National Parks Service guide to Native American activities, "Young boys followed each other down a very difficult path. The boys did not hang on to each other in this game. If one of them stumbled or fell, he had to go to the end of the line. This sort of game would develop strength, sure-footedness, and agility."

Follow the Music

Recreation centers, summer camps, and senior citizens' facilities often introduce music to the Follow the Leader game, which then evolves into dances like the conga line, snake, train, or the Finnish dance *letkajenkka*, which closely resembles the American dance known as the bunny hop from the 1950s.

FOX AND HOUNDS

ALSO KNOWN AS
Chalk Chase, Fox
and Geese, Hashing,
Hounds and Hare,
Paper Chase, Witch
in the Woods, Wolf
and Sheep

With deep historical ties to hunting, running, and hide and seek, versions of Fox and Hounds have been enjoyed by children and adults for centuries. By combining social bonding with exercise, the game has maintained a level of popularity not shared by many lost games of the past.

"It is not only a recreation, but a splendid exercise that keeps the blood from stagnating," said an article in *Harper's Weekly* magazine in 1874 that included a detailed illustration of a gaggle of boys, the "hounds," leaping over a fence in hot pursuit of the "hares."

THE SETUP

BASIC IDEA
The fox hides and the
hounds give chase;
many variations exist

PLAYING AREA
Games for younger
children can be played
on open lawns or in
the snow; adult games
are often staged on
wooded trails.

EQUIPMENT
Chalk or paper
(optional)

AGES
5 and up

PLAYERS
3 or more

Modern variations have scaled back the game for children to fit into the average suburban yard, while the communal sport of hashing is contested by adults across miles of trails. The common elements, the hunters and the hunted, have nearly limitless possibilities.

How to Play

In the simplest form of Fox and Hounds, a player is selected to be the fox, who heads off first and hides. After an agreed-on period of lead time, the hounds must find the fox.

For backyard games involving young children, the boundaries can be limited to match the size of the players.

○ Sometimes, hounds hunt alone; other times, they hunt in packs.

○ Most typically, the hound who finds the fox becomes the fox in the next round.

○ In Paper Chase, the fox marks his or her trail with pieces of paper.

○ In Chalk Chase, usually contested in urban neighborhoods, the fox uses chalk to leave a trail on sidewalks and buildings.

Formed in 1867 on Wimbledon Common in southwest London, the Thames Hare and Hounds club is the oldest formal cross-country running group in the world. In the early days, the club staged long-distance Hare and Hounds contests. Today the club organizes all forms of races, both social and highly competitive, including the London Marathon.

Variation: Wolf and Sheep

This game requires a minimum of four players. Two players are chosen as sheepdogs, who lock hands in a triangle with another player, the sheep. The wolf tries to tag the sheep, while the sheepdogs, maintaining their grips on each other and the sheep, spin around and try to keep the wolf away.

Variation: Fox and Geese

In winter, players can trample a large circle into the snow that is divided into at least four equal sections by perpendicular paths. In this game, one person is the fox, the rest are the geese. In one version, the geese run all around the circle, staying on the outer path, while the hound, who can run in the interior paths, tries to catch them. The first goose caught then becomes the fox.

Or, the geese start out in the middle (the henhouse) and try to evade the fox while running to the outer circle and then returning to the center. A similar game can be played in fall using paths in fallen leaves.

RUNNER IN A RED DRESS

"Hashing" is a worldwide adult social phenomenon that began as a Hounds and Hare game in Kuala Lumpur, Malaysia, in 1938. In 1987, a young woman came to a hashing event in San Diego, California, but was told she could not join the run because of her attire — a red dress with high-heeled shoes.

Nonetheless, she ran the full six miles, making such an impression that the next year, the San Diego "Hash House Harriers" staged the first Red Dress Run in her honor. All runners wore, as you can probably guess, a red dress. Hundreds of Red Dress Runs involving tens of thousands of runners are now held annually all over the world.

«FLASHBACK VICTORIA«

Our game of Witch in the Woods was a blast to play at night in an area with lots of hiding places. We would establish a base and one person to be the "witch," who went off to hide. After a minute or so, the rest of us would then scatter from the base to find the witch.

Once the witch was found, the successful player sent out a signal, such as "Olly, olly, oxen free!", and all the players ran back to the base. The witch would then try to tag all the players before they got there. If the witch was successful, she or he got to play witch again for the next round.

101

GHOST IN THE GRAVEYARD

ALSO KNOWN AS
Bloody Murder,
Flashlight Tag,
Fugitive, The Witch
Ain't Out Tonight

Quite possibly the best of the myriad games that combine elements of tag and hide and seek, Ghost in the Graveyard has been a time-honored tradition for thousands of years. A reversal of the many tag contests that pit one person against many, this game puts the "it" player, the ghost or the witch, in control from the start, and because the rules of the game keep it moving nonstop, everyone gets exercise, everyone wins, and, ultimately, everyone enjoys a bonding experience offered by few other games. This is an

THE SETUP

BASIC IDEA
Find the ghost then run to home base without being tagged and turned into a ghost yourself

PLAYING AREA
An open area with lots of hiding places

EQUIPMENT
Flashlights (optional)

AGES
6 and up

PLAYERS
3 or more

activity that can consume hours of playtime on warm summer nights.

The relatively modern invention of flashlights can introduce a safety factor as well as add spookiness to the game. If you've ever pointed a light into the woods at night, you know the lurching shadows can create all sorts of illusions; with a light on, the seekers might be able to find the hiders more easily, but maybe not.

Rules of the Game

This is a "the-more-the-merrier" game, so begin by gathering up as many people of all ages as you can find. Designate the boundaries of the "graveyard" and also the home base, a patio or picnic table, from which all the action will begin. It's always fun at this point to tell a ghost story or two to set the mood — the scarier the better.

○ **Ghost in the Graveyard officially begins with the selection of the first ghost.**

○ **While the remaining seekers recite the game's ages-old chant, "One o'clock ... two o'clock ... three o'clock ..." up to "twelve o'clock," the ghost runs off to hide.**

- After the seekers reach 12, they shout, "Midnight! I hope I don't see the ghost tonight!"

- The players then head off, alone or in pairs, to look for the ghost, but also to keep from being found by the ghost.

- When a seeker finds the ghost, he or she hollers out "Ghost in the Graveyard," upon which all the players try to run to the home base before the ghost tags them.

- Any players tagged by the ghost on the way immediately become ghosts themselves.

- In the second round of the game, all the accumulated ghosts go off and hide, either together or in separate locations, while the remaining seekers give the chant.

- If, at any point in the game, the ghost catches a player off guard and tags him or her unannounced, the captured contestant hollers out, "John's a ghost" or "Sue's a ghost," and that round of the game continues.

- It's up to all the players to recall who is, and isn't, a ghost.

- The final person to reach home base without being touched by the ghosts earns the privilege of being the first ghost in the next round.

Ghosts of Ancient Greece

The ancient Greeks were among the first civilizations to portray ghosts as scary, haunting, and even evil creatures. They believed the spirit of the dead hovered near the corpse and therefore avoided cemeteries, especially at night.

The Greek trilogy *Oresteia*, first performed in 458 BCE, contains one of the first known literary references to a ghost. Named Clytemnestra, she was the wife who murdered King Agamemnon. The Greeks, according to ancient artwork, were among the first to play a hide-and-seek game with ghosts as a theme.

«FLASHBACK VICTORIA«

This is a great game to encourage kids to go out and be active on warm summer nights. Every scent and sound is heightened after dark, from crickets chirping to distant front-porch conversations that suddenly seem right next door.

And the real fun? That was finding that special hiding place, one nobody would ever figure out in a million years. You might share it with your best friend or that cute boy from the next block, or maybe you'd keep it to yourself.

GHOSTS IN THE 'HOOD

In the modern neighborhood game of Fugitive, the players, most often teenagers, are divided into fugitives and detectives. The goal of the game is for the fugitives to make it from start to end in a set period of time before getting caught by the detectives wielding flashlights.

No boundaries exist and, in some variations, the detectives are allowed to use bicycles or even automobiles in the chase. Neither blockading the destination by the detectives nor trespassing onto private property or other improper activity is allowed, though cell phones are typically permitted for communicating whereabouts among teammates.

105

HOOP TRUNDLING

Most North Americans over the age of 55 remember when playing with a hula hoop was far and away the most popular children's pastime. Although the craze died down in the 1960s, hula hoops have made a comeback and millions are still sold every year. But the predecessors of that toy, which has inspired modern dances and exercise crazes, have a history with children dating back to the earliest cultures of virtually all continents of the world; in those days, children ran beside the hoops in fields and on early roads.

THE SETUP

BASIC IDEA
Keep the hoop rolling
no matter what!

PLAYING AREA
Any smooth, flat
surface. A bumpy lawn
makes it more diffi-
cult to keep the hoop
upright and rolling
forward, but can pro-
vide a fun challenge.

EQUIPMENT
A wooden or plastic
hoop; ideally the rim
is chest-high to the
player

AGES
7 and up

PLAYERS
2 or more

One of North America's first books of games, *The Boy's Treasury of Sports, Pastimes and Recreations*, published in 1847, quotes the Roman poet Horace as saying "hoop rolling is one of the manly sports of our time"; however, thousand-year-old paintings depict young girls frolicking with hoops, too. The game has almost always involved a stick to drive the rolling hoop forward and keep it upright if it begins to tee-ter. Ancient Greeks called this stick the "elater," while the Romans named it the "clavis." Some cultures used heavy metal hoops that were steered with metal hooks, although this ver-sion of the game soon lost favor because of the rather obvious injury factor.

Still Rolling

The Cooperman Company of Bellows Falls, Vermont, has been manufacturing nineteenth-century replica wooden toys since the 1950s. Co-owner Patsy Ellis says, "Our belief is that simple, natural toys that are long lasting are worth making. With the hoops, in particular, it's really amazing to see children today play a game that was passed from the Greeks to the Romans, through the medieval and Renaissance eras, right up to today."

FROM GRASS TO PLASTIC

The earliest hoops for trundle races were made from grapevines and grasses by Egyptians at least 3,000 years ago. Seeing a bamboo trundle hoop in Australia in 1957 inspired the founders of Wham-O, Arthur "Spud" Melin and Richard Knerr, to introduce the first plastic hula hoop to the American marketplace in 1958. More than 100 million customers purchased the toy, priced at $1.98, in just its first year.

Trundling for Glory

The King's School, Cambridgeshire, England, holds a famous hoop trundle race each year to mark the refounding of the school in 1541 by King Henry VIII. Opened circa 970, the school is one of the world's oldest. The overall winners of both the boys' and girls' hoop trundle races keep commemorative wooden tankards in their possession for a year. That high honor makes the annual trundle "the most spirited contest of the school year," according to the school newsletter.

Variations

109

Rolling a hoop, or "trundling," sometimes combines running speed with hand–eye coordination in races or relays among one or more people. To win, it's just as important to develop deft skills with the stick as it is to be fleet of foot. Practice in this game is essential, but fortunately hoop trundling is an addictive form of athletic solitaire.

○ Set up an obstacle course where the hoop must pass between two rocks without touching either one, or around trees or other obstructions.

○ Boys seem to like the version where the object is to roll their hoop into the opponent's hoop with the goal of knocking it to the ground. It's most fun when entire teams square off in a full-blown hoop battle. The team with the final hoop standing wins.

- Another version involves one player rolling the hoop while another player aims an object through it. Balls, stick, acorns, rocks, or pine cones work great!

- A group of kids with just a couple of hoops can set up relay teams to compete on a straightforward back-and-forth course or a more complicated one with obstacles.

«FLASHBACK PAUL«

I have to admit that I've never had much success controlling hoops, either vertically or horizontally, but I was astonished at the ease at which my writing partner slipped into her hula hoop and made it spin for minutes on end. I'm certain Victoria could have gone on for hours. I figured that racing the hoops vertically would be more my speed, but I soon found trundling takes a special knack and lots of practice.

It brought back fond memories of racing my grandfather's discarded tractor tires down Reeves Road in Bradford, Maine. Those heavy, wide tires weren't nearly as difficult to balance, but they were nearly impossible to stop once you got them rolling.

HORSESHOES

Played for centuries before being standardized in England in 1869, horseshoes remains a serious sport and backyard bonding experience the world over. The best players are deadly accurate from 40 feet away, often achieving "ringers," in which the horseshoe lands with its arms wrapped around the stake, on upwards of 60 percent of their shots. Some of the best games, though, are played between grandparents and their grandchildren, with techniques and family stories passed through generations.

Regulation stakes are of iron or steel, one inch in diameter, and protrude 15 inches from the ground. Each one should be leaning approximately 12 degrees (3 inches) toward the other. The pits can be dug anywhere from 43 to 72 inches long and 31 to 36 inches wide.

THE SETUP

BASIC IDEA
Pitch the horseshoe at the stake and try to hit a ringer; closest one scores

PLAYING AREA
Lawn quality doesn't matter. The stakes are typically set 40 feet apart and leaning toward each other about 12 degrees, with 14–15 inches showing above the ground. Frequent players may wish to dig pits for the stakes.

EQUIPMENT
• 4 horseshoes
• 2 stakes

AGES
4 and up

PLAYERS
1 on 1, or 2 on 2

Hit a Ringer

A simple game at heart, the idea is to pitch the horseshoe so it hits the stake. Although the official game with its heavy metal implements might be considered somewhat dangerous, especially for young children, horseshoes can be enjoyed by the youngest of players using small plastic shoes or even homemade papier-mâché rings.

It's a wonderful game to build hand–eye coordination and also to teach early conflict resolution, because the shoe deemed closest to the stake is awarded a point on the way to 21 for a win. As the saying goes, "Closest only counts in horseshoes and hand grenades"; therefore, the scoring is often a matter of debate! (A ruler can come in handy for really close calls.)

Ringer

Rules. Stakes are pounded in the ground 40 feet apart in an official game, but can be closer together in a friendly contest. Smaller or younger players are permitted to throw from a shorter distance.

○ Each player tosses two shoes in a row per round.

○ The horseshoe must fall within the boundaries of the court.

○ The order of throwing offers no particular scoring advantage, but going second often provides a psychological advantage because you know the challenge in advance.

○ When pitching the shoes underhand along a line that stretches outward from one stake, players are allowed one step toward the opposite stake.

○ A shoe that lands within six inches of the stake is worth one point, while a ringer is worth three.

○ Points can be accumulated in each round or cancellation scoring can be used. That means that only the shoe closest to the stake earns a point. In other words, if both teams or players throw a ringer, no points are awarded. If both teams or players land shoes within six inches of the stake, only the shoe closest to the stake is awarded a point.

Strategy. Accuracy of shoe pitching takes loads of practice on the speed of the arm swing, the knee bend, the release point, and, most importantly, how to best hold the shoe. Some players hold it at the base, with the U of the shoe resting in the palm of their hand. Others hold the shoe sideways as a backward C. Whichever way you decide, learn to stick with it and establish a personal rhythm. It's always a good idea to warm up the back, legs, and arms before playing horseshoes. Repeatedly lobbing a heavy metal object 40 feet in the air may be more exercise than you think.

Variation: Chinese Horseshoes

A hybrid of cornhole (see page 51) and Cherokee marbles (see page 42), the game of Chinese horseshoes is played using six hockey pucks or metal discs and two playing surfaces with three holes each, known as "pits." A player or team has the option of rolling, throwing, or bouncing its three pucks toward the pit.

Pucks that go in the closest hole score two points, the middle hole four points, and the farthest hole six points. Pucks that land on the surface of the pit, which measures 18 inches wide by four feet long, score one point.

As in cornhole, players have the right to try to knock pucks away from holes, which are four inches in diameter. If both players or teams land a puck in the same hole, they cancel each other out. Games are played to 31, but players can win instantly by scoring a "yack-a-pooh," which is tossing all three pucks in the three different holes on the same turn.

A horseshoe hanging as a talisman on the wall, chimney, or door is considered lucky in most cultures around the world. Many people believe that the horseshoe must be pointed upward to be considered fortunate; a downward-facing horseshoe allows the luck to run out!

KICK THE CAN

ALSO KNOWN AS
Tin Can Alley, Tip the Can, Turkey Lurky

An exciting combination of hide and seek and tag, this relatively modern variation of a game with ancient themes was once a staple activity in neighborhoods across the United States. Similar to Capture the Flag, it can be played on lawns, in alleys or streets, or on school playgrounds, provided, of course, that safe hiding places are nearby and plentiful.

The object of the game is for the "it" player to find all the other players and put them in jail. Depending on the number of players involved, this can take a long time, because if a free

THE SETUP

BASIC IDEA
The "it" player spots
hiders and races them
to kick the can and get
them out

PLAYING AREA
An open area with plenty
of nearby hiding places

EQUIPMENT
A can, bucket, or milk
carton; anything that will
fly a reasonable distance
when kicked

Note: Using a ball makes
it tough for the "it"
player. We think players
should stick with tradi-
tion. It's more fun to kick
an actual can!

AGES
3 and up

PLAYERS
3 or more

player beats the "it" player back to the can,
all other players are released from jail to go
hide again.

How to Play

The game begins when players mark a central
base or "jail" in an open area. Just about anything, from a picnic table to a Frisbee to a hula
hoop to a baseball glove lying on the ground,
will serve the purpose. Another area fairly close
by is selected as the location of the can, which
can be a bucket, a paper or plastic milk carton,
or a small cardboard box. It's also a good idea to
determine boundaries so that hiding players are
not allowed to go too far away.

An "it" player is chosen by any appropriate means and the game begins any number
of ways. Sometimes one player kicks the can
and scatters with the rest of the players to
hide while the "it" player retrieves the can and
returns it to its original position. Another way to
begin is to simply have the "it" player close his
or her eyes and count to 50 or 100.

○ **The "it" player then tries to find the hiding
players.**

- When a player is spotted, the "it" player calls out the name and location ("Sally behind the tree") and then races her back to the can.

- If Sally gets there first, she kicks the can and then goes to hide again. If the "it" player reaches it first, Sally must go to the jail area.

This can be a fun game to play with multiple "it" players, but set the rules so that one of them can't spend the entire game defending the can area. Timing the game can also be fun: every player must make at least one run for the can within a certain period of time, or run the risk of being disqualified when time runs out. This is one of those games where "olly, olly oxen free" or another catchphrase is used to bring in players who are still out hiding.

Strategy. Daring players may break for the can at any time during the game if they feel they can kick it before getting caught and going to jail. Players quickly learn the notion of risk/reward; a hiding place nearby keeps you close to the can, but potentially easier to spot.

A hiding area farther away might keep you safer longer, but it can be hard to win a race back to the can from a great distance.

118

Tin Can Alley

British merchant Peter Durand patented the tin can for food packaging in 1810. The first tin cans for beverages were used by the Gottfried Krueger Brewery of Newark, New Jersey, which delivered Krueger Cream Ale to beer drinkers in Richmond, Virginia, in 1935. Pepsi, still in its infancy, was one of the first emerging brands to test soft drinks in cans in 1948, but Coca-Cola waited until 1962 to adopt the process nationwide.

KICKBALL

ALSO KNOWN AS
Kick Baseball,
Soccer Baseball

Enjoying a resurgence of popularity, the American game of kickball is truly a sport, not just a game, for all ages. By applying the same basic rules of baseball and using a soft rubber ball unlikely to cause injury to players, buildings, and windows, kickball retains the universal appeal that it has had on playgrounds since World War I.

Many young children, who often master the ability to kick way before they gain the skill to throw accurately, are drawn to kickball as a way to learn the intricacies of three outs per

THE SETUP

BASIC IDEA
Kick the ball and run around the bases back to home while the other team tries to get you out

PLAYING AREA
A baseball field is ideal but any large, flat area will work.

EQUIPMENT
• A soft rubber ball
• Objects to mark home plate and 3 bases

AGES
4 and up

PLAYERS
Officially 8 per team, but a backyard game needs at least 4 people

inning, balls and strikes, running bases, and catching a ball. Some children never quite embrace baseball and softball, perhaps out of the fear of being hit with a hard ball or the humiliation of swinging and missing time after time. Some adults, secretly or not, share those same anxieties, which kickball eliminates.

The result is a game that can be enjoyed as a family activity among players of all ages, or as a more organized sport complete with umpires, uniforms, and scorecards. Official leagues are found worldwide, but the greatest games are the ones where a little girl or boy makes it to first base for the first time.

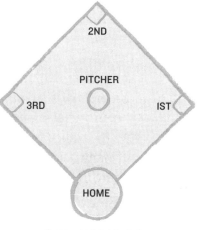

Suggested field of play

Rules of the Game

The fundamental rules of kickball are nearly identical to those of baseball or softball, with one notable exception: The team in the field can throw the ball at the kicker, still called a "batter," to get him or her out as long as the ball hits below the neck. That's why official kickballs are large and soft, inflated to only 1.5 pounds per square inch of air pressure.

Games can be played on a standard Little League or T-ball field, or any large back lawn or playground. An improvised diamond can be set up with three bases and home plate; the pitcher's mound can be anywhere from 20 to 45 feet away from home plate. The limits of the outfield can be delineated as either outs if the field is short or home runs if the field is large enough to accommodate the leg strength of the players.

○ **Pitchers can either roll or bounce the ball to the batter, but the ball can't be higher than a foot or so off the ground when it reaches home plate.**

○ **In some games, balls and strikes are called; in family games, players usually can make contact on just about every pitch.**

WORLDWIDE

What began as a few folks enjoying the sport around Washington, D.C., in the mid-1990s evolved into the World Adult Kickball Association (WAKA), founded by a quartet of college friends. WAKA leagues involve tens of thousands of players 21 or older in several nations.

Kickball player and author Christopher Noxon calls the participants "rejuveniles," which he defines as "eternally young grown-ups," who almost always schedule a trip to the local pub after a match.

121

When a player kicks a ball and someone in the field grabs it, the biggest decision is whether to throw the ball directly at the batter or to throw it to the teammate covering a base.

Rules can easily be accommodated for games with fewer players.

In a game of three against three, for example, "ghost" runners usually factor into the outcome.

Bunting may or may not be allowed.

A fairly complete set of rules for "Kicking Baseball" was set out by Emmett Dunn Angell in his 1910 book Play: Comprising Games for the Kindergarten, Playground, Schoolroom and College.

Ramping It Up

Eric Heiberg thinks traditional kickball, where people must wait their turn to "bat" and players sometimes stand in the outfield for an entire game without fielding a ball, is far too sedentary; therefore, the full-time computer programmer and part-time comedian from Austin, Texas, invented mojo kickball, which adds elements of tag and dodgeball.

In his game, played by "mojonauts," six kickballs of different colors are in play at any one time. Runners are guarded by "chasers," who try to prevent them from being tagged out. With unlimited outs, strikes and foul balls, a referee is essential to keep track of it all!

KUBB

A thousand-year-old Swedish game, kubb (rhymes with tube) is an interesting blend of bowling, ring toss, and team strategy. It has, thus far anyway, resisted overt migration to North America, but that will change if a University of Wisconsin student has anything to say about it.

Minnesota native Carl Schroedl received a classic wooden kubb set from a cousin in the village of Hälsingland, Sweden, during a family reunion in 2002. Schroedl soon became a missionary intent on spurring what he calls a "kubbolution."

THE SETUP

BASIC IDEA
Knock down your opponent's kubbs and then knock down the central pin

PLAYING AREA
Commonly played on lawns and in public parks; Scandinavians play on ice

EQUIPMENT
- 10 rectangular blocks (6 inches high)
- 1 large rectangular block (12 inches high)
- 6 batons or dowels (12 inches long)
- 4 pegs or other boundary markers

AGES
5 and up

PLAYERS
Teams of 2 to 6 players

"As a sophomore in high school, I wrote about kubb for an English paper," he says. "People were interested. Pretty soon we started playing it every day at lunch, and then other kids in school played it at lunch, too. Then there were clubs and tournaments." When Schroedl went to college, he helped launch the kubb craze there.

"Nothing against croquet or bocce or horseshoes," he said. "But this game is just more interesting with far more strategy, even though it involves some of the same skill sets. Kids love it, and they can also play it with their parents and grandparents. It's the kind of game, sort of like golf, where no matter how good you get, there's still an element of luck that keeps it interesting."

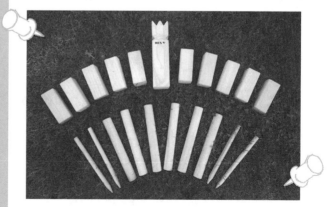

Take Down the King

The ultimate object of kubb is to be the first to knock down the "king," a foot-long block of wood in the middle of the playing field, but first you have to upset all five of your opponent's kubbs — toppling the king before knocking down the others automatically loses the game. To knock down the blocks you toss six batons, which are foot-long dowels.

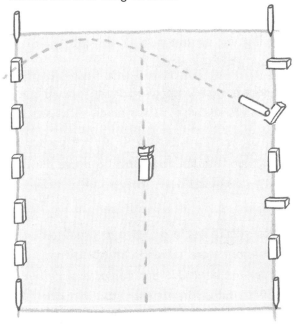

The official measurement for a field is 5 × 8 meters (about 15 by 25 feet), but it can vary depending on age and skill of players.

FACT OR FICTION?

A popular Scandinavian folktale perpetuates the likely myth that kubb originated with the Vikings, who some considered to be vicious pillagers. As the story goes, the Vikings whittled their own kubb game pieces out of the skulls and bones of their victims. A more likely theory holds that medi-. eval Swedish woodsmen devised the game for their children; kubb literally means "block of wood" in Swedish.

Rules. This is a simple game at its core, but with a fairly complex set of rules and some skill required, it is more challenging than it might seem. On the other hand, it's easy to play a simplified version of the game with a 5-year-old in the living room. Wherever you play, it's addictive fun for all ages.

- Players toss a baton at the kingpin; the one that lands closest without knocking it down goes first.

- Members of a team take turns tossing the batons, dividing them evenly and rotating as necessary to ensure that all have equal turns.

- The baton must be tossed underhand so that it spins vertically; overhand or sideways throws are not allowed.

- The simplest rules state that once a kubb is knocked down, it is out of the game. The first team to knock down all five of the other team's kubbs and then knock down the king, wins.

- More commonly, the game is played so that any knocked-down kubbs are tossed onto the opponent's side of the field, where they must be

The highest quality wooden kubb sets in North America are said to come from the hands of Amish and Mennonite craftsmen in Shippensburg, Pennsylvania. Many of their ancestors settled in Sweden after religious persecution in Europe in the 1500s and the game was passed down through generations of woodworkers.

knocked down again (for a total of 10 kubbs) before the king can be attacked.

○ Still other variations involve "bowling" the kubbs to knock down the opponent's kubbs.

Strategy. A game with strict adherence to international tournament rules can take two teams of two people an hour or more to play; for a backyard game, the rules can always be modified to move things along. It takes a fair amount of skill to accurately toss the batons so that they knock down the kubbs, especially if you set up the field according to the official size of 5 by 8 meters. Outdoor play can be quite competitive, with a lot of near misses and jockeying for position.

The Russians have a similar game known as gorodki. In this game, players or teams each set up a "village" of 15 wooden objects. Players then take turns tossing "bats" at the objects and the first team to destroy the other's village wins. In some cases, players reportedly use actual baseball bats!

127

Kubb International

With a recent surge in the popularity of kubb, the island of Gotland — the largest landmass in the Baltic Sea, 55 miles from the Swedish mainland — has held the annual Kubb World Championships in August each year since 1995. More than 200 teams from around the world participated in 2010, with more than a dozen different countries represented, including the United States, England, Germany, Italy, and Japan.

LACROSSE

ALSO KNOWN AS
Baggataway,
Intercrosse, Lax

Known as "the fastest game on two feet," lacrosse has emerged as the most popular game of many that originated with Native Americans; in the past few years, it has become the fastest-growing sport in the United States. A goal-oriented game like soccer and field hockey, lacrosse's primary distinguishing feature is a stick with a webbed pouch at one end used to catch and propel the ball forward. The other requisites to play well include speed, agility, footwork, and teamwork, all of which make the game

THE SETUP

BASIC IDEA
Using sticks with small nets, throw the ball from player to player while advancing it toward the goal

PLAYING AREA
A large, smooth open area

EQUIPMENT
- A ball
- A stick for each player
- A framed goal area

AGES
6 and up

PLAYERS
2 on 2, up to 12 on 12 or more

ideal for the primary goal of combining fun with exercise.

The best players can throw the ball more than 100 miles per hour and sprint like the wind, but lacrosse can be easily enjoyed by players of all ages as a lawn or beach game. Simply tossing the ball back and forth is a great way to get used to the equipment and hone one's technique.

Field size can be adjusted to accommodate the age, number and ability of players, and rules — especially about contact — become important when safety is an issue. With the exception of games involving well-protected players wearing the proper equipment, hitting with the sticks is never allowed.

Rules & Strategy

The object of the game is to score the most goals, but the challenge is keeping possession of the ball down the length of the football-size field while running or passing until a shot can be attempted. An essential skill is "cradling," which is the equivalent of dribbling in basketball or hockey. Rocking the stick with your

arms and wrists as you run creates enough centripetal force to hold the ball in place in the webbed pocket of the stick until you're ready to release it. Generally, right-handed players place the right hand highest on the stick and the left hand at the base.

Another key skill is learning to efficiently scoop up balls on the ground. The best players will tell you that's where games are won and lost. The trick is to bend down low, with your back and stick parallel to the ground. After collecting the ball, you usually must pass quickly, because another player will almost always be in pursuit.

«FLASHBACK PAUL«

We had a shed roof at our house that was only slightly pitched and ideal for practicing catching, cradling, and throwing skills. For those times when no friends or family can be found for practice, find a roof or wall and practice, not just lacrosse, but all throwing and kicking skills. It's during these solitary times, when no one is watching or critiquing, that a kid can really develop a personal comfort zone with the equipment and game. Of course, it's always a good idea to have permission and be sure not to crack anyone's siding or windows.

This pair of **Menominee wooden lacrosse game sticks** are carved with intricate designs. One of the lacrosse balls is made from animal skin and the other is carved from hardwood. Compare to modern equipment on the facing page.

BACK IN TIME

Though versions of lacrosse have been played by Native Americans for centuries, the modern game was discovered by Jesuit missionaries from France who witnessed the Iroquois Indians of what is now upstate New York and southern Ontario playing what they still call *baggat-away.* The French thought the sticks resembled bishops' crosiers and imme-diately called the game "la crosse."

Montreal's Olympic Club organized what is believed to be North America's first non-Indian team in 1844 and a Canadian dentist, George Beers, published official rules of the game in 1867.

131

Rooting for the Iroquois

Though they are credited with inventing the game, the six tribes of the Iroquois Confederacy — the Onondaga, Mohawk, Seneca, Oneida, Tuscarora, and Cayuga — were restricted from playing in international lacrosse competition until 1990. The Iroquois Nationals placed fourth in the world in 1998, 2002, and 2006, but were again restricted from participating in 2010 when the United States and England could not agree on the legitimacy of the Iroquois passports.

The team was heartbroken, according to Oren Lyons, an Onondaga clergyman and former player. "When you talk about lacrosse, you're talking about the lifeblood of the Six Nations," he said. "The game is ingrained into our culture and our lives. This is our game and our gift to the world."

LADDER TOSS

ALSO KNOWN AS
Blongo Ball, Bolo Ball, Hillbilly Golf, Ladder Ball, Ladder Golf, Monkeyball, Rattletail Toss, Snake Toss, Tailgate Golf

A close cousin of horseshoes, cornhole, quoits, and other underhand-throwing contests, ladder toss is a descendant of a game played by both Native Americans and cowboys out on the range. In that version, the players held live snakes by the tail and flung them toward a fence post or tree limb. Points were scored if the snake wrapped around the fence or limb.

No Snakes Needed

Today's version uses bolas (two balls connected by a short piece of rope) instead of snakes. The object is to toss the bolas so that they wrap around the rungs of the target. Points are scored depending on which rung is hit and trying to knock your opponent's bolas off the target is part of the game.

Although the complete components of the non-snake version of the game can be readily purchased online or at toy and sporting goods stores, an old painter's ladder works just fine, and DIY tinkerers can easily cobble together ladders from dowels, pipes, or tubing. Ladders typically have three rungs, although homemade versions can be built with any number of rungs. Perpendicular bases fastened to the bottom keep the ladders upright.

For the game's double ball, also known as a "bolo," "bola," or "bolas" many players drill holes through golf balls and connect them with a thin rope or thick string that is knotted on each end. In addition to being less expensive than the manufactured models, the homemade sets offer something money can't buy: a comfortable "home court" advantage from knowing your own equipment. (For another game played with bolas, see Double Ball, page 72.)

Rules. If you've ever tried throwing a bolas underhand toward a horizontal bar, you know the apparatus travels end over end through the air; if thrown in the right direction at the proper height, it hooks and grabs the bar. You also know the bolas can be quite unruly!

To throw the bolas, start with one ball in your hand and let the other one dangle with the connecting rope running through your fingers. Standing about five paces away, lob the ball underhand, the same way you would a bocce ball, toward the ladder.

Ladder toss equipment is easy to make; this version uses PVC piping and some old golf balls.

135

○ The official game calls for three bolas to be thrown per player or team per round.

○ Games are usually played to exactly 21 points. In the event of a tie game at 21, extra rounds are played until one team or player is leading by at least two points.

○ Scoring is one point for a bolas that hangs onto the lowest rung, two points for the middle rung, and three points for the top rung.

○ If all three bolas land on the same rung, or one bolas lands on each of the three rungs, an extra point is awarded. The maximum number of points per inning is 10.

Strategy. As in bocce and cornhole, knocking the other player's bolas off a rung is part of the fun strategy of the game. Some bolas wrap themselves multiple times around a rung and are virtually impossible to dislodge. Others land on a rung but just dangle from it. Those are relatively easy to knock off with a well-placed shot. But risk/reward comes into play here, because knocking off an opponent's bolas makes it almost impossible to land your own bolas on the rung.

Monkeying Around

After playing a game his father called monkeyball on a camping trip in 2003, Andy Frushour came back to his East Lansing, Michigan, home and, as he said, "took the game to the next level." The physical education organizer formed monkeyball leagues, special events, and even computerized rankings of the world's top 100 players.

The annual Monkeyball World Championship, held each year at "The Old Orchard" on Route 99 between Lansing and Eaton Rapids, Michigan, draws dozens of players from 10 states. The game is ladder toss at its core, but monkeyball players call their ladders "trees" and throw the bolas from a full 30 feet away.

It sounds simple, but the aspect of having to score exactly 21 points really makes this game challenging, because the lowest rung of the ladder, although only worth one point, is probably harder to hit than the other two rungs. If one player or team in the game charges off to a big lead of, say, 20–10, the low-scoring team still has a good chance of winning.

The double ball for ladder golf is based on the bolas or boleadoras used by the ancient **Chinese** and **Native American** tribes for hunting. The weighted balls or stones connected by cords were used to entangle animals' feet so they couldn't run and were easy to capture.

LONDON BRIDGE

ALSO KNOWN AS
King George's
Troops, Oranges
and Lemons,
Stone Bridge

Based on folk songs and nursery rhymes that may be close to a thousand years old, the game of London Bridge and its cousins have largely been relegated to antiquity in recent decades, possibly because it's too docile for our hyperactive X-Games culture. The words, "London Bridge is falling down, falling down, falling down; London Bridge is falling down, my fair lady," still roll off the tongue, but the associated actions in the Victorian game are often seen as too old-fashioned by all but the youngest of modern youth.

THE SETUP

BASIC IDEA
Two players form an
arch and try to capture
other players as they
pass through

PLAYING AREA
Any area free of trip-
ping hazards

EQUIPMENT
A rope, if a final tug of
war is part of the plan

AGES
3 and up

PLAYERS
At least 6, but the more
the merrier

That view needs to change. A deeply symbolic game inextricably linked to a familiar song, London Bridge teaches early elements of dance and rhythm. As a social activity that de-emphasizes winning and losing, the game offers a healthy modicum of exercise either indoors or out. It can also be used to introduce new languages and cultures, since the fundamental "falling bridge" lyrics have been translated the world over.

How to Play

139

The game begins with two players facing each other and forming a bridge by locking their hands together in the air above their heads.

- As the bridge players sing, "London Bridge is falling down . . . ," a train of children, holding on to each other's waists, passes under the arch.

- As the verse is finishing, ". . . falling down, my fair lady," the bridge players lower their arms to try and capture the player who happens to be passing through.

- Captured players must leave the line until only one remains.

Any games that involve music enhance the opportunity for communal bonding and this one, especially, fills the bill. The arches, whether two players or several, can share knowing glances and instantly increase the tempo of the song, or conversely, slow it down depending on who they want to catch. Words can be changed or added to the original London Bridge song, first published in the 1700s.

London Bridge is falling down, falling down, falling down;
London Bridge is falling down, my fair lady.

How shall we build it up again, up again, up again?
How shall we build it up again, my fair lady?

Build it up with wood and clay, wood and clay, wood and clay;
Build it up with wood and clay, my fair lady.

Wood and clay will wash away, wash away, wash away;
Wood and clay will wash away, my fair lady.

And continuing:

Build it up with silver and gold/Gold and silver I have none.

Build it up with needles and pins/Pins and needles bend and break.

Build it up with stone so strong/Stone so strong will last so long.

Variations

In some versions of the game, the prisoner is led, still confined by the arms of the captors, to the "prison" and asked, "Will you have a diamond necklace or a gold pin?" or an equivalent question. Two prison keepers represent either the necklace or the pin and the prisoner lines up behind whichever one he or she selects. The game then continues, "London Bridge . . . my fair lady," until all the players are caught and aligned behind a prison keeper.

In some games, a final team of winners is chosen by a tug of war between the necklaces and the pins; the bridge players can join one side or the other to ensure even teams for the tug. This part of the game, in many cultures, holds rich symbolism, as though the players are pulling lost souls back from the afterlife.

Another way of playing has the captured players joining the bridge rather than standing behind prison guards. That way, the bridge becomes an expanding tunnel as the game progresses, making it increasingly challenging to pass through without getting caught. The final player left outside the clutches of the bridge is the winner.

LOST IN TIME

The origin of the London Bridge game and folk song is still a matter of great debate. According to Walt Disney's *The Truth About Mother Goose* (1957), the song refers to the deterioration of the London Bridge that was built in 1176 and demolished on July 4, 1823.

Others say the song is older than that, inspired by the destruction of the London Bridge by Olaf II of Norway during the war of 1014. Still others believe the game and song originated in Denmark under the name of "Bro, Bro Brille."

141

A crossing has existed at approximately the same spot along the Thames River in London since about 55 CE, when the Romans constructed a bridge atop wooden pilings.

In 1831, King William IV and Queen Adelaide dedicated a bridge that served until it was sold to American magnate Robert P. McCulloch of McCulloch Oil for $2.5 million in 1968. That London Bridge, shown below, was rededicated on October 10, 1971, at Lake Havasu City, Arizona, where it still stands.

MEXICAN KICKBALL

ALSO KNOWN AS
Indian Kickball, Kick
Croquet, Kickball
Racing, Rarajípari

A primitive racing contest with more ties to soccer than traditional kickball, this pastime dates to the ancient Tarahumara (TAH-rah-oo-MAH-rah) Indians, who are said to have invented it thousands of years ago in the mountains of northwestern Mexico. To this day, the Tarahumara, which translates to "foot runners," start running great distances at very young ages, always kicking a ball along the way.

Scaled-down versions of rarajípari are played in Mexican villages and at fiestas across North America on courses that are modified to fit into neighborhoods, playgrounds, and backyards.

THE SETUP

BASIC IDEA
Be the first to kick a small ball over a distance or through an obstacle course

PLAYING AREA
Can be flat or hilly

EQUIPMENT
• 1 or 2 small balls, such as tennis balls
• Stones, stakes, or other objects as obstacles

AGES
3 and up

PLAYERS
2 or more

Kick and Run

The simple goal is to kick a ball around a course faster than the other player or team. Winners can be determined by stopwatches or the more traditional method of racing to see who crosses a finish line first.

Rules. Three primary versions of the game exist. The traditional contest rewards endurance, while the modern game emphasizes speed. The backyard and playground version is typically set up as an obstacle course.

Mexican kickball can be played one against one, but it's more fun with multiple players.

○ **For races involving a team, the captains agree on a starting and finishing line.**

○ **The captain kicks the ball forward and the other players race toward the ball, trying to advance it toward the finish line.**

○ **Some rules call for all players on the team to kick the ball in succession, meaning no team is faster than its slowest runner.**

Strategy. Long kicks advance the ball quickly, but also run a greater risk of going off target. The tennis balls typically used in this game don't lend themselves to accurate long kicks.

In versions of the game set up as obstacle courses, players might be required to kick the ball over a box, under a picnic table, around a lamp post, over a bench, and through a goal at the end. Relay races are really fun in this format. Soccer coaches can also use this style of game as a drill in practice to emphasize ball control and kicking dexterity.

≪FLASHBACK PAUL≪

This game takes me back to the neighborhood on Edward Street in Waterville, Maine, in the 1960s and early '70s, where we could make a game or race out of *anything*. We kicked ratty tennis balls around the elementary school, then crossed the street and kicked them toward the Thibodeaus' dance studio, around old Mr. Howard's house and through his backyard, under our fence, and finally through the old barn door at the end of our dirt driveway. Four decades later, I can remember every detail of that neighborhood as if I had been there yesterday.

Native Americans throughout the southern United States and northern Mexico have long considered kickball racing to be a spiritual activity. Races of 30 miles or more are contested in the autumn after ceremonial feasts during which that season's runners are named by the tribal leaders. Traditional balls are still formed from stone or, more often, mesquite or wood from the paloverde tree.

145

MÖLKKY

Games that involve knocking down sticks with other sticks trace back to the world's earliest civilizations. Anyone can play and the implements for the game are easily crafted from branches and small logs. Various versions of more formal games of skittles have been played across Europe since at least the Middle Ages, including the sport of kyykka (pronounced KEE-ka), which involves flinging a baseball bat–like implement at the sticks.

THE SETUP

BASIC IDEA
Knock down numbered pins to add up to an exact score of 50

PLAYING AREA
Any flat surface; bumpy lawns make the game tougher!

EQUIPMENT
• 12 numbered wooden pins or skittles (approximately 8 inches high and 3 inches in diameter)
• A thick dowel or small log for throwing (8 to 12 inches long)

AGES
4 and up

PLAYERS
2 or more

It All Adds Up

In the mid-1990s, a Finnish toy company vastly increased the skill and strategy needed for the game by painting a number from 1 to 12 on top of a dozen pins or "skittles." The object of Mölkky (pronounced MUL-kih), or modern Finnish skittles, is to be the first player or team to score exactly 50 points by knocking down the appropriate number of pins. Exactly 50 is the key. If you score more than 50 points, your total reverts back to 25 points.

The math component makes this an ideal game to reinforce addition and subtraction skills, while the requirement of an exact point total takes this game well beyond the strategic realm of "whoever scores the most points wins." For that reason, we think this version of an ancient game deserves to be a worldwide classic.

147

The Finnish Mölkky Association organizes the annual world championships, which attract hundreds of teams from across Europe to compete in Lahti, Finland.

Rules. The game begins with all 12 pins or skittles packed tightly together, somewhat as pins would be at a bowling alley. The pins are generally placed in four rows, with pins 1 and 2 in front; 3, 10, and 4 in the next row; 5, 11, 12, and 6 in the third row; and 7, 9, and 8 in the back row. Players stand 10 to 12 feet away and the first player lobs a dowel or small log at the pins.

Pin setup

The scoring is what makes the game really interesting:

○ **If a player knocks down a single pin, he receives the total painted on the pin.**

○ **But if the player knocks down multiple pins, he or she receives one point for each pin knocked down. So, for example, if the first player knocks down all 12 pins, he or she receives 12 points.**

○ **Any fallen pins are then placed upright in the exact spot where the bottom of the pin landed and the next player throws.**

○ **As the game advances, the pins can become quite spread out.**

- If a player misses three times in a row, he or she is eliminated from the game.

- As a player or team approaches 50 points, say 45, then the goal would be to score only five points by knocking down the 5 pin, or maybe the 1 and 4 pins; however, if a player knocks down the 6 pin by mistake, the score would revert to 25.

Strategy. Having to keep a running count of your points makes for all sorts of angling and strategy. Pads of paper can be used to keep score, but the requirement of keeping track in your head can help build some rudimentary math skills.

Because the tossing dowel rolls freely and is fairly long, this game is tougher than it looks. Unlike bowling, where strength, coordination, and keen aim determine success or failure, Mölkky is all about planning ahead as you approach the coveted 50 points. Because strength doesn't offer any particular advantage in this game, it's great for the young and old, even those confined to wheelchairs.

149

Scaled Down

The Finnish company Tuoterengas, which owns the trademark on the name Mölkky, recently introduced "TupaMölkky" or Table Mölkky, which can be played indoors. The only difference from the outdoor game is that the playing pieces are smaller.

QUOITS

Some historians debate about which toss game came first, horseshoes or quoits. We're going with the quoit, a metal donut-shaped weapon used by the ancient Greeks and Romans. The earliest versions, known as chakrams or war quoits, were thrown sidearm, and the most skilled warriors could decapitate an enemy from a great distance. Soldiers were said to have come up with the idea of sticking a stake in the ground and tossing their weapons underhand toward the target and the game of quoits was born.

THE SETUP

BASIC IDEA
Toss a set of rings toward a stake, scoring points for landing the nearest to or over the stake

PLAYING AREA
Frequent players often construct a pit around the hobs, although hammering the hob directly into the lawn works just fine. Note: Official quoits leave divots when they land.

EQUIPMENT
• Four quoits (regulation ones are metal)
• 1 stake (hob), driven into the ground to a height of about 4 inches

AGES
2 and up

PLAYERS
2 or 4

According to Peter Brown of the National Quoits Association in England, the sport of horseshoes emerged as a poor man's alternative. "Quoits were quite prized and were, in fact, often the trophy for winning a match," he said. "Commoners who did not have access to quoits took up tossing old horseshoes instead."

How to Play

Most people today know the game as ring toss, which is played with metal or rope rings lobbed toward a plastic, wooden, or metal stake, called the hob. Infants often have plastic rings in their cribs and senior citizens' homes usually keep wooden ring toss sets in the recreation room; however, for the purists, only the metal equipment and ancient rules will suffice.

We believe that quoits is a better family game than horseshoes simply because players of all skill sets are more likely to be rewarded. Unlike horseshoes, which can be dominated by highly skilled players hitting ringers, landing a quoit directly over the hob is rare. That brings strategy and blocking more into play, much as with bocce or croquet.

151

Rules. Scored similarly to horseshoes, quoits involves landing the ring over, on, or near the hob.

○ Players or teams alternate throwing their pair of quoits.

○ The simplest scoring awards three points for a ringer, two points if the ring is touching or leaning on the hob, and one point for the closest quoit to the hob.

○ If two players ring the hob during the same round, only the quoit on top scores points, bringing heartache to the player who gets "topped."

○ In team play, players need to be careful not to outdo their own teammates and waste good shots.

○ The first player or team to 21 points wins that round.

Games can be played with just one hob, but official rules call for two, spaced 21 feet (6.5 m) apart. The throwing distance can easily be modified when younger or less-skilled players are involved. The U.S. Quoiting Association calls for quoits to weigh 4 pounds each with a diameter of 6.5 inches and a 3-inch-diameter hole in the center. For children's ring-toss sets, of course, the weight will be far less, and homemade versions of the game can be played by creating rings out of twigs, ropes, thin wood, or any other pliable material.

The Only Place for Quoits

Sporting goods stores in the United States routinely sold metal stakes and rings for quoits until the 1920s, when George May from Akron, Ohio, made national headlines for his prowess in horseshoes. May's ability to hit ringers with up to 60 percent of his shots, according to newspaper accounts, fired up the nation's interest in horseshoes and pushed quoits out of the public consciousness. Today, the only official rings for quoits in the United States are forged by Amish workers in Lancaster, Pennsylvania.

THE KING SAYS NO

Although he came to power as a boy in 1377, King Richard II left his mark on game history when he banned the playing of quoits and other games in England because he considered them to be a distraction from the important work of daily life. Though by all accounts it was seldom observed, the ban remained in place for nearly five centuries until Queen Victoria officially lifted it in 1845.

153

In England, quoits pitches are often located behind the village pub.

Karl Smith founded one of the nation's largest quoits tournaments on his lawn in East Coventry Township, just outside of Pottstown, Pennsylvania, in 1990. His turf features 10 sets of pits ready to accommodate up to 30 teams and more than 100 players. The U.S. Quoiting Association runs the National Quoit Tour with cash prizes of about $12,000. Virtually all the nation's best players live near Pottstown, where the game retains one of its few pockets of widespread popularity in the United States.

RED LIGHT, GREEN LIGHT

Often one of the first outdoor games introduced to very young children, Red Light, Green Light and its international variations are a wonderful way to induce laughter and introduce mild competition to the backyard or playground. A modicum of adult supervision can be useful at first, but then stand back and let the little minds take their first crack at group leadership and conflict resolution. It's amazing what happens.

THE SETUP

BASIC IDEA
Players try to tag the "cop," whose back is turned, freezing in place when he or she turns around

PLAYING AREA
Any surface will do

EQUIPMENT
None required, though chairs and clothing can be added

AGES
3 to 10

PLAYERS
At least 3, but the more the merrier

Rules & Strategy

In the classic version, one player, in some cases a teacher or adult, takes the role of the "cop" while all other players line up a reasonable distance away. Their goal is to run up and touch the cop without him or her ever seeing the other players move.

- To begin, the cop faces away from the players, with eyes closed, and hollers out "green light."

- At any point, the cop can holler out "red light" and spin quickly around.

- Any players who the cop sees still moving are told to go back to the starting line or may even be eliminated from that round. Because it relies on the honor system, the issue of whether a player is still moving is always subject to debate.

- The "green light," "red light" commands continue until one player reaches and touches the cop. In most cases, that player then plays the role of cop for the next game; however, it can also be agreed on in advance that all players will take a turn playing cop.

It's easy to make the game a bit more complex. For example, place one or two chairs on the lawn with the rule that a player must sit in a chair before he or she is eligible to touch the cop. Scatter articles of clothing, such as hats, gloves, and/or coats, around the lawn for players to put on before they can advance.

Other fun variations can include additional commands by the cop, such as "green light hop," in which case all the players have to advance forward by hopping instead of running, or "green light skip," or "green light left foot," after which the players hop forward on just the left feet. These variations help keep this simple game interesting for older children.

. . . .

In England, where this game is known as Grandmother's Footsteps, the "it" player typically says a nursery rhyme before turning around. In some cases, the player is allowed to do this under his or her breath so other players can't hear it.

. . . .

RED MEANS STOP

The standard of "green means go" and "red means stop" began in 1868, when the first traffic light was installed in London. The gas fixture reportedly exploded less than a year later, injuring the constable who was manning the manual controls.

157

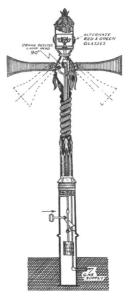

This design for the first street crossing lights in London was modeled on railway signals.

RED

D ROVER

Perhaps no game in this book evokes more conflicting, yet indelible, memories among those of us above a certain age than Red Rover. This game, which was a staple activity at playgrounds around the world for at least two centuries, is now at the epicenter of the debate about how much parents and caregivers should attempt to protect children from themselves.

The issue is that this good, clean, fun game is somewhat violent at its core. The teams stand facing each other hand-in-hand in two human chains, and when one team calls out "Red

THE SETUP

BASIC IDEA
Players link hands to form two lines; opposing players try to break through the line one at a time

PLAYING AREA
The softer the playing surface, the better, because players do fall down.

EQUIPMENT
Absolutely nothing

AGES
5–10 works best; older, heavier children may be more prone to injury

PLAYERS
At least 3 per side; the more, the better

Rover, Red Rover, send Johnny over," Johnny charges full speed toward the other team. Success is when he breaks the chain by overpowering two players from the opposing team, forcing them to lose their grip on each other. Imagine if Johnny is, say, 150 pounds and the two players trying to keep him from breaking through weigh a combined total of 150 pounds.

That's where the potential for injury comes in and that's why, at many schools from coast to coast, Red Rover is no longer allowed on the playground. To some adults, Red Rover is nothing more than tackle football without a ball and pads; to others, the loss of Red Rover symbolizes an overly mandated and regulated childhood.

How to Play

The group is divided into two lines that face each other from some distance apart.

- By mutual agreement, one team goes first, calling for an opposing player to charge their line.

- If Johnny does break through the chain, or "octopus," he chooses one person from the opposing team to take back with him to join his original team.

- If Johnny fails to break through, he becomes part of the opposing team and joins the chain at the point where he tried to break through.

- This process of "Red Rover, Red Rover, send (name) over" continues back and forth until all the players form only one chain.

A few supervisory adult safety checks will maximize the fun and minimize the injuries: 1) players in the chain should hold only hands and not lock wrists and arms. The locking technique can cause more serious injury; 2) all players should be about the same size; and 3) players should not be allowed to raise their joined hands above chest height so that runners are not "clotheslined" at the neck and jolted to the ground.

Because all the players are on the same team at the end, fans of the game stress that everybody wins. The purists feel that this should easily satisfy the caregivers who believe sports and games are all about participation and not about the scoreboard.

This game also teaches great teamwork and consideration, because a winning team captain will know to pair a stronger, larger player next to a weaker, smaller player for support. An important adage in life and business is that a team is only as strong as its weakest player; this game reinforces the concept of team cooperation from a young age.

A More Peaceful Version

The Japanese play a nonviolent form of Red Rover, called *Hana Ichi Monme.* Rather than sending someone over to physically break the chain, the children sing a song in unison. When the song ends, the team captains compete in a *janken,* a version of Rock, Paper, Scissors. The winner goes back to his or her team, which huddles to determine which player to select from the other team. The game ends when all the players wind up in one line.

SEND RED ROVER OVER

No one seems to know for certain where the name Red Rover originated, except that in the days before widespread construction of bridges in the eighteenth and nineteenth centuries, a red rover was the name for a shuttle boat in the river. Red rovers were also nurses who would bring aid to both sides in a conflict, sort of a historical precursor to the Red Cross.

161

SACK RACE

ALSO KNOWN AS
Gunny Sack
Race, Potato Sack
Race, Three-
Legged Race

A classic example of how children can turn *anything* into a contest, sack races have been around, in all likelihood, for as long as humans have made sacks — about 20,000 years, according to archeologists. Sack races can be contested with the participants carrying the sacks over their shoulders, or more popularly, wearing the sack over one or both of their legs and hopping or crab-walking to the finish line.

The most fun races of all, guaranteed, are the ones requiring teamwork, such as the

THE SETUP

BASIC IDEA
Climb in a sack and hop
to the finish line

PLAYING AREA
Soft ground to break
the inevitable falls

EQUIPMENT
Potato or grain
sacks, pillowcases,
or large, heavyweight
plastic bags

AGES
5 and up

PLAYERS
2 or more

three-legged race, or relays with multiple players but only one sack per team. If you've ever tried to pull a sack on or off quickly in the middle of a race, you know how silly things can get.

A company in Virginia (see Resources, page 202) sells traditional burlap bags in sets of four, eight, or twelve and publishes a set of formal rules for sack races. Other companies have supplanted the burlap with vinyl or plastic and have even sewn handles on the bags for better ease of maneuvering, an innovation at which the purists would surely scoff!

163

A Sack of Coal

The tiny English village of Gawthorpe spawned a variation of the sack race in a pub where three coal miners were boasting about who could run up a hill fastest with a 50-kilogram (110-pound) sack of coal on his back. In 2013, the World Coal Carrying Championship will celebrate its 50th anniversary sponsored by the Westgate Brewery.

164

VARSITY SACK RACING

In the late 1800s, sack races were included in most collegiate track and field meets, and international sack races were conducted in St. Louis, Missouri, during the 1904 World's Fair, although they did not count as an official event for the third summer Olympics held concurrently with the fair.

On May 1, 1929, Johnny Finn of Brooklyn, New York, set the world record in the 100-yard sack race in 14.4 seconds.

How to Play

A simple sack race is fairly straightforward: The players stand in their bags, hold up the sides with their hands, and try to hop or waddle to the finish line faster than the other players. In the three-legged version of this race, two players share a bag and each puts one leg inside the bag and one leg outside. The challenge in this race is to coordinate leg movements with the other player without falling. Practicing in advance is strongly advised!

«FLASHBACK VICTORIA«

Ah, burlap potato sacks! Every kid should experience the simple joy. It's a great game to play with a lot of kids at once.

When you were little, the sack would practically devour you, but what fun! To win required great athleticism and cardiovascular fitness, but the most fun part was the sack relays, where you had to strip out of your own sack and then help get your partner into it. Sometimes we'd fall down from laughing so hard.

Variation: Relay Races

In relay races, the sack handoff becomes a critical factor. One teammate must shed the bag and assist his or her teammate in getting the bag on quickly. In a three-legged relay, which requires a minimum of four participants per team, getting two players out of a sack and two other players into the same sack usually brings moments of hilarity.

For a truly fun but far more complicated version of the race, teams of three or more people connect like a human sack chain. Three players require two sacks; a team of five would require four sacks, and so forth. Racing requires coordination of movement among several people, making the camaraderie far more significant than the race outcome.

165

The burlap used to make the classic potato sack is made from fibers of the fast-growing jute plant. A large-leafed species native to Bangladesh and India, it is seeded in standing water during the monsoon season each year.

SCAVENGER HUNT

ALSO KNOWN AS
Hot and Cold, I Spy,
Map & Compass,
Treasure Hunt

A game unlike any other in this book, scavenger hunt engages the intellect at least as much as physical prowess. Identifying and finding items, either hidden or in plain view, can be an exhilarating experience when multiple players and teams are competing against each other and/or the clock. Extra challenges, from compass and map reading to botanical identification of plants, can turn the average backyard into a life sciences laboratory where the real experiment is how to have the most fun while learning new things.

THE SETUP

BASIC IDEA
Find items on a list —
the possibilities are
endless

PLAYING AREA
Can be played any-
where, including urban
neighborhoods

EQUIPMENT
Can be existing items
in the yard or items
hidden by adults

AGES
5 and up

PLAYERS
Any number

Anything Goes

With no clearly defined right or wrong way to play, players and organizers of scavenger hunts can let their imaginations run free. For example, a hunt might include public performances: hide a microphone wrapped in an instruction sheet that commands players to sing "Mary Had a Little Lamb" before proceeding to the next item.

Or each team might use a digital camera or cell phone to photograph their findings, especially if the items are not meant to be moved or collected. Older kids can play at night with a flashlight, which always adds a level of intrigue and fun.

Rules. Scavenger hunts can be played in almost infinite ways.

○ In timed contests, individual players or whole teams can be assigned categories such as trees, flowers, seeds, or a set of objects of a certain color or shape. Identifying and finding the most of each category in a set period of time leads to a winner.

167

○ For scavenger hunts in which identical lists of items are involved, it can be fun to have opposing team members conceal the items; the hiding becomes just as enjoyable as the seeking.

○ Some scavenger hunts might have no list at all; the instructions can simply be to collect the 10 most interesting items you can find and then let an appointed judge determine the winner. In these days of heightened environmental awareness, the game can be a race to collect the most trash or recyclable items.

Hand-drawn maps are always fun to include in a scavenger hunt. The addition of a map helps children understand spatial relationships and develop a sense of direction such as left or right, east or west. Excitement invariably builds as teams approach the final treasure, which can be a special prize or just the bragging rights associated with winning.

Variation: Hot and Cold

In the game of Hot and Cold, the hider — often a parent or caregiver — aids the seekers with verbal clues as to the whereabouts of the treasure. "Warm" means that he or she is getting close; "cold" conveys heading in the wrong direction. For younger children, it's fun to turn this into a vocabulary game with more descriptive adjectives. "Searing," for example, means the hunter is practically touching the object; "frigid" means not even close. This game can also introduce new languages. In French, "froid" means cold and "chaud" means hot. In Spanish, it's "frio" and "caliente," and in, say, Croatian, cold is "hladan" and hot is "vruce."

168

Variation: Nature Hunt

Use a scavenger hunt to teach children about plants in the most fun way possible. All it takes is a quick jaunt around the yard to compile a list of items — oak leaf, maple leaf, dandelion flower, strawberry blossom, moss, fern, lichen — for the kids to collect.

For really young children, you can draw a quick picture or map, or print out photographs so they can match the items. As the children get older, the maps and items can become more complicated. For example, not just an oak leaf, but a pin oak leaf, which is far more narrow and pointed than a white oak leaf, or not just any fern, but a Christmas fern, with evergreen fronds in a classic tree shape.

169

170

Find a What?

Probably the most famous scavenger hunt in the United States and one of the largest in the world was founded in 1987 by five University of Chicago students. The subject of two documentary films, the four-day "Scav Hunt" involves scouring North America for a predetermined list of more than 300 items, public performances, and a road trip of up to 1,000 miles that begins at the Reynolds Club along 57th Street in the Windy City. Among the more unusual items to have made the list, and been found and brought to campus, are a piping hot, fully glazed ham, a painting on velvet titled "Dogs Playing Dungeons and Dragons," a Stradivarius violin (extra points for a cello), and a live armadillo.

SEPAK TAKRAW

ALSO KNOWN AS
Kick Volleyball,
Net Footbag, Net
Hacky Sack

At its most polite and docile version, footbag or hacky sack involves players standing in a circle and passing a beanbag ball or sack back and forth with their feet. Initially popularized in this country at Grateful Dead concerts in the 1970s, the highly social game has become a staple activity at American playgrounds and street corners within the past three decades.

THE SETUP

BASIC IDEA
Kick a lightweight
ball over the net —
no hands allowed

PLAYING AREA
A large smooth area; be
aware that this game is
brutal on lawns!

EQUIPMENT
• A lightweight ball
• A badminton net, set
5 feet high (lower for
less competitive play)

AGES
8 and up

PLAYERS
2 on 2, up to 6 on 6

Look, Ma, No Hands!

A traditional Southeast Asian sport that has been around for at least 500 years, sepak takraw — sepak means "kick" in Malay, and takraw is "ball" in Thai — takes the hacky sack and adds elements from martial arts, soccer, and volleyball. Played on a badminton-sized court with a net, the rules are roughly similar to those of volleyball with one major exception: hands cannot be used to advance the ball back and forth over the net.

The addition of a net elevates this game into a sport and advances the elements of skill, strategy, athleticism, and exercise. The best players are typically whippet-thin and in amazing physical condition, capable of full 360-degree whirlwind spins in the air from a standing position — but the rest of us can play a kinder, gentler game, provided we master at least some of the necessary footwork!

Rules. A traditional sepak takraw ball is constructed of woven rattan about 5 inches in diameter. These days, soft woven plastic balls are most common, and beginning players can easily make their own out of newspaper and duct tape. The ball shouldn't bounce too high or hurt players if it hits them.

- Games are played to 21 and points are awarded whether a team is serving or receiving.

- As in volleyball or badminton, a team scores a point when the ball hits the ground within the opposing team's court.

- If the served ball lands outside the court, the other team receives the serve.

- If the ball lands outside the court and the opposing team touched the ball last, then the serving team gets a point.

- Teams can play the ball only twice before advancing it over the net on the third kick.

- A player can advance the ball by bouncing it once off his or her head or chest before kicking it.

- Serving is done in rotation, but nonserving players can stand anywhere on the court.

GAME OF THE GODS

King Naresuan of Ayutthaya, who ruled Thailand from 1590 to 1605, is said to have enjoyed the game, and in Bangkok, a 1782 mural at the nation's most cherished shrine, Wat Phra Kaew (the Temple of the Emerald Buddha), depicts the Hindu god Hanuman playing sepak takraw in a ring with a troop of fellow monkeys.

173

The ball is traditionally made of woven rattan.

Strategy. It's usually best to have the players with the best kicking and leaping ability near the net, especially if they have mastered the "roll spike," an upside-down kicking technique that propels the ball back over the net at speeds of more than 100 miles per hour! (Kids, don't try this at home!)

As with so many games, sepak takraw can be played by a couple of kids on a patch of dirt or at the level of international competition.

Sepak takraw has been contested as a sport at the Asian Games since 1990 and a campaign is underway to persuade the International Olympic Committee to add the sport. More than 20 countries, including the United States and Canada, now have national associations with representatives on the board of the global governing body, the International Sepak Takraw Federation.

TUG of WAR

ALSO KNOWN AS
Rope Pulling,
Tug of Peace

This purest of contests, as old as time, could not be simpler to play. You take your end of the rope and I'll take mine. We'll both pull with all our might; one of us will win, one will lose. Yet of all the games in this book, tug of war probably competes with Red Rover as having the worst image in today's America.

Seen as too competitive, too dangerous, and too potentially harmful to self-esteem, the simple act of going *mano a mano* on opposite ends of a rope has been banned from many school grounds for the past 20 years or so. Even in

THE SET UP

BASIC IDEA
Teams take opposite ends of a rope and try to pull each other over a centerline

PLAYING AREA
A smooth, open area (the grass may get a little torn up!)

EQUIPMENT
A sturdy rope that won't break

AGES
3 and up

PLAYERS
At least 2

schools where it's allowed, some administrators would have the players call their game "tug of peace."

Enough, already! It's time to loosen the noose around this game. One of the great games for teaching teamwork and team pride — and even rewarding the big kid who is perhaps heavier than his or her average classmate — tug of war should be played by today's youth just as it has been for millennia. We are all for adult supervision, of course, so grab a rope and pull!

Ready, Set, Pull!

As with many children's games that have been commandeered by adults, this one has official rules and associations. National and international competitions are often eight on eight, for example, and dictate official footwear so players don't gain an unfair advantage (see note on the 1908 Olympics on page 179).

In the backyard or playground game, though, the most important role of the adult is to make sure the children have a safe rope that won't snap and send players on both sides flying backward. Short of that happening, the worst injuries related to tug of war (or peace) are the occasional rope burns that come from soft hands pulling too hard; however, even those rarely happen if the tug of war is contested among players of similar weights and ages. Gloves help, too!

One safety note for caregivers and adult playground monitors is to have players on each end of the rope alternate, with one player gripping from the right side and the next player in line gripping from the left side. This helps eliminate crashes if the rope is suddenly pulled forward. And never allow any player, even the player at the end of the rope, to tie the rope to any part of his or her body.

AN ANCIENT GAME

Carvings and drawings indicate that versions of tug of war have been around for at least as long as recorded civilization. In Korea, children wrapped their arms around each other's waists with the players at the front gripping each other's hands. In ancient Afghanistan, players pulled on a wooden stake rather than a rope.

That's One Big Rope!

The Naha Tsunahiki, held each year in Naha, Japan, holds the dual distinction of employing the world's largest natural rope for the world's largest tug of war contest. Thousands of people from the west side of the city tug against thousands from the east side, trying to drag a 600-foot rope made of rice straw that weighs more than 44 tons and measures 5 feet in diameter.

When the contest is finished, a citywide celebration ensues, but not before everyone pulls out a pocket knife and slices off a good-luck souvenir for the coming year.

179

Tug of war was an official Olympic sport from 1900 to 1920, with 1908 showcasing an especially bitter fight between the United States and Great Britain. The British players, nearly all police officers wearing heavy boots with steel heel plates, easily held their positions in the grass at White City Stadium in London. The U.S. delegation protested vehemently, but ultimately, Britain's finest swept the gold, silver, and bronze medals.

VOLLEYBALL

VOLLEYBALL

ALSO KNOWN AS
Beach Volleyball,
Fistball, Jungle Ball

In any given week, volleyball is enjoyed by some 800 million people around the world. Although it was invented in the United States more than a century ago, the game exploded in status after American success in beach volleyball in the 1996 Atlanta Olympics. Kent Steffes and his legendary partner, Karch Kiraly, won the gold medal and captured the American imagination.

Since then, municipalities, homeowners' associations, and private homeowners have dug their own pits, filled them with sand, and

THE SETUP

BASIC IDEA
Teams serve and
return a ball over a net,
scoring points if the
other team misses

PLAYING AREA
A smooth, soft lawn

EQUIPMENT
• A ball
• A net (or rope)
• Boundary markers

AGES
5 and up

PLAYERS
2 on 2 to 6 on 6,
or more

fashioned their own beach courts in their back-yards. For most of us, though, volleyball is the quintessentially perfect lawn game.

Dig, Set, Spike!

Volleyball has loads of rules, covering things like how the ball can be hit — with an open or closed first, or off the head or feet. In backyard games, some of these are made up as the game goes along, but the general idea is to advance the ball over the net in such a way that the other team cannot return it within three hits.

All you need is a soft bouncing ball and a rope tied between two posts or trees for the makings of an afternoon of fun. Of course, a bevy of companies stand at the ready to supply you with a regulation ball and net, which the official rules will tell you must be exactly 7 feet, $11^{5}/_{8}$ inches off the ground.

In your yard, you can make the net any height you like, play the game with a kickball or a beach ball, and invite Grandma, Uncle Charley, and all the kids to join in. For a family activity where everyone will get some exercise, few games rival volleyball.

181

Rules. The official court size is 30 feet wide by 60 feet long, but those dimensions can be modified depending on the number and size of players, not to mention the size of your yard. Teams are typically six against six, or two against two for beach volleyball, but an informal game can include any number of players. Official games are played to either 15 or 25 points, but again, that's flexible in home play.

○ The game begins with a serve from behind the end line of the court, which is divided in half by a net or rope.

○ Servers continue serving as long as their team scores points. The serve changes whenever the receiving team scores a point.

○ If the serving team serves or hits the ball so that it lands inside the boundary of the opponent's court, the serving team scores a point and serves again.

○ If the serving team serves or hits the ball and it doesn't go over the net or lands outside the boundary of the opponent's court, the opposing team scores a point and receives the serve.

○ If a player touches a ball before it goes out of bounds, the opposing team scores a point and receives the serve.

○ The ball may be hit by three players on one side before being returned, but cannot be hit by the same player twice in a row.

○ A player may play the ball off the net but may not touch the net; if so, a point is awarded to the opposing team.

Players are generally required to rotate the serve from player to player on a team, and also rotate their position on the court. In some games, players can stand anywhere on the court after the serve. Taller players are usually positioned closest to the net.

Variation: Fistball

Europeans originated a game similar to volleyball known as fistball or faustball that has been contested for at least 1,800 years. The court is much larger — 60 feet wide and 150 feet long — although the service line is closer to the net than in volleyball.

In fistball, the ball is allowed to bounce once on the lawn between each hit, but only three

PARTNERS IN FUN

Although Canadian Dr. James Naismith is known the world over for having invented basketball at Springfield College in Massachusetts in 1891, a lesser-known fact is that his friend and colleague, William Morgan, invented volleyball only four years later. As the director of physical education at the Young Men's Christian Association in Holyoke, Massachusetts, Morgan was looking for a game that could be enjoyed by a population older than those playing Naismith's basketball. He originally called his invention "mintonette."

hits are allowed before the ball must advance back to the opposite side of the net, which is only six feet off the ground. Games are played to 11 points.

As the name would indicate, the ball must be hit using a fist and not an open hand; however, advancing the ball off any part of the arm is allowed. Fistball is a huge sport in many nations, which compete for a World Championship every four years.

" LEARN THE LINGO "

Bump Passing with the forearm

Dig Passing a ball close to the ground

Set When one player passes the ball so that another player can spike it

Spike A ball hit hard on a steep angle

BEACH VOLLEYBALL has spawned its own colorful jargon, including:

Beer When a hard-hit ball lands between a defender's legs

Hubby & Wife When a serve is directed straight down the middle between two players, who are paralyzed by indecision about who should hit the ball

Jumbo shrimp A shot hit over the head of the defender to a far corner that lands in bounds

WHEELBARROW
RACE

ALSO KNOWN AS
Crab Legs Race

The wheelbarrow is a simple machine that has been around since the time of the ancient Greeks. For children, a ride in a wheelbarrow from a willing adult can represent a racecar, a chariot, or a sailboat. Turning themselves into human wheelbarrows is a pastime that has amused generations of bored kids. It can be awkward and exhausting, especially for the "wheelbarrow," but it's always a barrel of laughs for everyone involved.

THE SETUP

BASIC IDEA
The "wheelbarrow" walks on his or her hands while a partner holds his or her legs

PLAYING AREA
The flatter and smoother, the better; even with actual wheelbarrows, this isn't a game for pavement!

EQUIPMENT
Wheelbarrows (optional)

AGES
4 and up

PLAYERS
4 or more

Ready, Set, Go!

At its core, the wheelbarrow race is a simple first-to-the-finish-line contest to be won by the fastest, strongest players; however, all sorts of rules and configurations can add twists and turns, thereby adding to the thrills and occasional spills of the game.

Obstacles and relays are great additions to the race and some players have turned the transfer of positioning into an acrobatic art form. Rather than simply dropping the teammate's legs to the ground and assuming the position of wheelbarrow, the most nimble players perform a double summersault while still holding on to the teammate's legs. The end

result is that the original wheelbarrow is now standing and the standing player becomes the wheelbarrow. It's one of those moves where practice makes perfect.

Variation: Use a Real Wheelbarrow

If the kids are older and stronger and you have more than one wheelbarrow available, races involving actual wheelbarrows are lots of fun. Try adding obstacles to the racecourse so that the effort requires as much dexterity in steering as it does in running.

If it's a two-on-two race, make the race from point A to point B and back again, with the players switching places halfway through. The speed of the exchange becomes a fast and furious factor in the race. When more players are available, relays can be great fun and help to take the emphasis off any one player's strength or weakness.

Still another variation of the wheelbarrow race has one player holding each handle of a wheelbarrow containing a load of some sort, perhaps even another player or two. The level of balance and cooperation required among all the players overshadows strength and speed.

Guinness World Records recognizes Australian sprinter Otis Gowa as holding the record for the fastest 100-meter wheelbarrow run. On May 15, 2005, Gowa pushed 110-pound Stacey Maisel over the grass at Davis Park at Mareeba, Queensland, Australia, in 14 seconds. Guinness also crowned a group of 1,378 students in Singapore in 2009 for setting the record for the largest wheelbarrow race, with 689 teams.

187

How Far Did You Say?

Perhaps the longest wheelbarrow race in American history began December 8, 1878. Offering a purse of $1,500 to whomever could trundle a wooden wheelbarrow from San Francisco to New York City the fastest, newspaper publisher George Hearst found willing takers in R. Lyman Potter of New York and Leon Pierre Federmeyer of France.

Besting Potter by an estimated 1,000 miles, Federmeyer wheeled into New York City on July 23, 1879. Having passed through California, Nevada, Utah, Wyoming, Colorado, Kansas, Missouri, Ohio, and Pennsylvania, the well-celebrated pedestrian was estimated to have traveled 4,500 miles.

WIFFLE BALL

ALSO KNOWN AS
Junk Ball, Lawn Ball,
Stick Ball

Technically speaking, the great American pastime of baseball is a lawn game — if you have a very, very large lawn with no picture windows, planters, and innocent bystanders. That's because the nearly rock-hard ball is notorious for breaking things . . . lots of things. That difficulty led David N. Mullany, a former semiprofessional baseball pitcher from Shelton, Connecticut, to devise a plastic ball and bat for his 12-year-old son in the early 1950s.

THE SETUP

BASIC IDEA
Played like baseball or softball but with a light plastic bat and slotted ball

PLAYING AREA
Any grassy area where 3 bases and a home plate can be set up

EQUIPMENT
• A plastic bat (or thick, straight stick)
• A Wiffle ball (or a round wad of paper, cloth, or elastic bands)

AGES
4 and up

PLAYERS
1 on 1 to teams of 9 or more

After experimenting with several variations, Mr. Mullany came up with the now-famous Wiffle Ball, a white sphere with slotted oval holes on one side, named for the "whiffing" or striking out that often happens when players swing wildly at the ball, which curves easily and unpredictably. More than a half-century after its invention, at least a half-dozen imitators manufacture plastic baseballs and bats, but scarcely anyone calls the resulting game anything other than Wiffle Ball.

With tens of millions of players of nearly all ages and worldwide leagues, the Wiffle Ball craze shows no signs of abating. At its core remains the game of stickball: a piece of a tree limb or a broom handle and some paper, rubber bands, or cloth bunched up and bound into a ball is all you need for a one-on-one game of toss and hit, or a full sandlot slugfest.

How to Play

The official game rules of Wiffle Ball roughly mirror baseball, but call for "ghost" runners and award singles, doubles, triples, or home runs depending on where the ball lands. House rules typically dominate backyard games to accommodate varying lawn sizes and the proximity of fences and neighbors, as well as the ages of the players.

Many backyard versions of the game do allow for base runners, for example, who can be called or tagged out in several ways, among them:

○ A player in the field catches a batted ball in the air.

○ A player in the field catches a ball that has hit the ground and throws it to a teammate covering the base before the runner arrives.

○ A player throws the ball and hits the base runner before he or she arrives safely at the base. (This method is predictably frowned on by many adults and should be monitored if older, stronger players are competing against younger players.)

Before Wiffle Ball, kids played stickball in the streets.

191

A MAN OF MANY TALENTS

Whether baseball was really invented in Cooperstown, New York, will forever be debated. The English claim that baseball derives from their sport of rounders and a group of Manhattan dwellers were reportedly playing a game of "town ball" long before Abner Doubleday, a major general in the U.S. Army, was credited with developing baseball around 1839. The accomplished General Doubleday, whether he invented baseball or not, did fire the first shot in defense of Fort Sumter in the opening battle of the Civil War, and he also patented the cable car railway system of San Francisco.

General Abner Doubleday

Wiffle around the World

Although star baseball players including Ted Williams and Pete Rose were once spokesmen for the Mullany family's new game in the 1950s and 1960s, the arrival of the Internet has caused the popularity of Wiffle Ball to explode since the mid-1990s, even without advertisements. Go to *www.wiffleball.org* for details on the World Wiffle Ball Championship, which attracts more than 170 teams each year.

Five Prized Pavement Games

Many of the games described in this book can be played anywhere on lawn or pavement, though some are particular to the softer surface of turf. Here we briefly highlight a few classic playground games that just don't work on grass. But any safe sidewalk or driveway surface will do.

1. ROMAN BALL

All you need is chalk and a bouncy ball and at least a couple of players, although the more the merrier. Draw one circle two to five feet in diameter inside of another larger circle 10 to 15 feet in diameter depending on the size of the players.

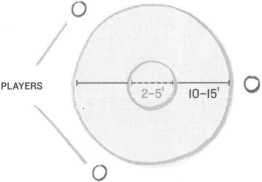

PLAYERS

2–5'   10–15'

All players stand outside the outer circle and the player with the ball must bounce the ball so it bounces inside the center circle and outside the outer circle. If a player standing outside the circle catches the bounced ball before it hits the ground, the catcher gets a point. If the ball isn't caught, the bouncer gets a point and gets to bounce it again. Players are free to change their positions outside the circle to anticipate where the bounced ball will land.

If the ball misses the inner circle or doesn't reach outside the outer circle, the bouncer loses a point, but keeps bouncing the ball until a player catches a ball and earns the next turn. The first player to obtain a certain number of points is the winner.

2. TIC-TAC-TOSS

Combine tossing skill with tic-tac-toe strategy in this great game for all ages. Simply draw out a tic-tac-toe board on the driveway or sidewalk and find pebbles, bean bags or some other implement to toss from a reasonable distance. If a player lands a pebble inside a square, that player can mark the square with an X. The opposing player then tries to land the pebble in another square and mark it with an O. If pebbles land on the chalk lines or outside the board, a player loses his or her turn. The first player with three Xs or Os in a row is the winner.

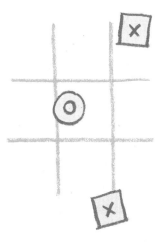

3. THE RUNWAY GAME

In this team game, one blindfolded player (the
pilot) can move but not see and the other teammate (the air-traffic controller) can see but not
move. The object is to help the blinded player
navigate along a predetermined length of sidewalk or driveway without stepping on objects
which have been strewn along the "runway"
by players from the opposing team or teams.

Balls, rackets, clothing, cardboard boxes,
and so on all work great as obstacles. Proper
commands are essential, such as "take two
short steps in my direction" or "take one long
step to your left." If the pilot "crashes" into an
object, he or she must start over or let the other
team have its turn.

195

4. STOOPBALL

Also known as porch ball or the doorstep game, this game can be
played as solitaire, or with two or more players in front of any set
of steps (where the owner will allow!). Any bouncy ball will work,
although tennis balls or small rubber balls are most common. A player
begins by tossing the ball at a set of stairs. Catching the rebound after
one bounce is worth five points and catching the rebound in the air is
worth 10 points. If the ball bounces twice, or just rolls back toward the
thrower, no points are scored and the player gives up his or her turn.

The best score of all is obtained when the ball hits exactly on the
edge where the horizontal step meets the vertical riser and bounces
back toward the thrower who catches the ball in the air. This occur-
rence, known as a "pointer" is worth 100 points. Games are often
played to 500 or 1,000 points.

5. HOPSCOTCH

Perhaps the quintessential pavement activity, this game dates to the seventeenth century. One of a variety of different numerical patterns is drawn on the pavement with chalk and games begin when markers are tossed onto squares 1 to 9. Hoppers pounce from squares 1 to 9 and then back again, stopping to pick up their marker along the way, being careful to land within the squares and to not lose their balance.

"Do the Math" is an educational variation for older children in which the board is drawn to resemble a calculator. Each jumper must take three jumps in succession, with the end result adding up to the desired number. For 1, for example, the jumper might land on the 2 then the minus sign then the 1. To score 6, the hopper could land on 3 then the multiplication sign then the 2. The variations, in other words, are only limited by imagination.

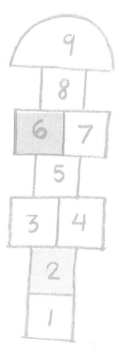

197

WE WANT YOU TO KNOW ABOUT . . .
Helping Children:
the Annie E. Casey Foundation

When I was eight years old, my foster mother, Agatha Armstead, enrolled me in a classical ballet school where my interest and passion in the arts was nurtured. Not only did I learn how to do a pirouette, but the discipline required in ballet became a fundamental force in my life, conditioning me for many opportunities as well as challenges still ahead.

I often wonder what would have become of me without Agatha's support. Studies show that children who are exposed to the classical arts and team sports at an early age acquire life skills that are instrumental in their personal growth and development. In 1990 I started a charitable organization, the Rowell Foster Children's Positive Plan, to offer scholarships to help children in foster care thrive through participation in fine arts classes, sports and summer camps, and cultural enrichment activities. I also serve as a national spokesperson for the Annie E. Casey Foundation (*www.aecf. org*), the direct charity arm of United Parcel Service, as well as Casey Family Services (*www.caseyfamilyservices.org*).

My goal is simple: to help children who would otherwise not have a chance to reach their full potential, striving to offer these youth the same long-term commitment and opportunities that foster parents, social workers, and mentors can provide. I believe that exposing them to these various disciplines at an early age enriches their lives more than we know, by providing invaluable structure, support, and encouragement.

I am proud to say that many of the children we have helped have gone on to careers in the arts and hundreds of other successful pursuits. Children everywhere need our help more than ever to reveal the hidden possibilities of life on this glorious planet. We all need to do what we can, from nudging them off the couch and outdoors, to encouraging them to pursue higher education, to ultimately making the same kind of dreams come true that Agatha made possible for me.

— **Victoria Rowell**

AND . . .
The SafeLawns Foundation

I can't recall when lawns and fields were not a significant part of my life. Whether playing primitive games on the lawn as a toddler, assisting my grandfather in harvesting hay for the cows as a young boy, or mowing lawns for clients during my teenage years and well into adulthood, grass has probably always been more on my mind than the average guy's.

By the mid-1990s, however, I found myself in a doctor's office receiving a severe diagnosis: acute chemical sensitivity. The cause, according to the physician, was exposure to the chemical weed and insect killers I had used on customers' properties. Since that time, I've been on a mission to let North American homeowners know about the health and environmental risks associated with these dangerous types of products — many of which are banned in much of Canada and other countries.

In 2006 and 2007, I took my anti-pesticide advocacy to another level with the formation of The SafeLawns Foundation and the publication of my first book, *The Organic Lawn Care Manual*. At *www.safelawns.org*, information is published almost daily about how to care for lawns without dangerous pesticides and how to advocate for safer lawns, parks, and playgrounds in your communities. *The Organic Lawn Care Manual* is full of tips about how to create a beautiful lawn naturally, so that when you send your children outside to play games, the toxicity of the grass is the least of your worries!

— **Paul Tukey**

Resources

BADMINTON

USA Badminton
http://usabadminton.org

World Badminton
http://worldbadminton.com

BOCCE

**Collegium Cosmicum
Ad Buxeas**
http://bocce.org

**United States
Bocce Federation**
630-257-2854
www.bocce.com

CAPTURE
THE FLAG

**U.S. Scouting
Service Project**
BOY SCOUTS OF AMERICA
http://usscouts.org/usscouts/
games/game_cf.asp

CHEROKEE
MARBLES

Cherokee Nation
918-453-5000
http://cherokee.org

CORNHOLE

**American Cornhole
Association**
http://playcornhole.org

**American Cornhole
Organization**
888-563-2002
http://americancornhole.org

**World Bean Bag
Association**
708-425-5454
http://thewbba.com

CROQUET

**United States Croquet
Association**
561-478-0760
www.croquetamerica.com

DODGEBALL

**National Amateur
Dodgeball Association**
847-985-2120
http://dodgeballusa.com

National Dodgeball League
952-931-0404
http://thendl.com

DOUBLE BALL

Native Wellness Institute
http://nativewellness.com

**Traditional Native
Games Society**
406-226-9141
http://traditionalnativegames.org

FIELD HOCKEY

Planet Field Hockey
http://planetfieldhockey.com

U.S.A. Field Hockey
http://usafieldhockey.com

FLAG FOOTBALL

United States Flag & Touch Football League
440-974-8735
http://usftl.com

United States Flag Football Association
http://usffa.org

FLYING DISC

Disc Golf Association
831-722-6037
www.discgolfassoc.com

Freestyle Players Association
http://freestyledisc.org

USA Ultimate
800-872-4384
www.usaultimate.org

World Flying Disc Federation
http://wfdf.org

HASHING (FOX AND HOUNDS)

http://half-mind.com

HOOP TRUNDLING

Cooperman Fife & Drum Company
802-463-9750
http://cooperman.com

HORSESHOES

National Horseshoe Pitchers Association of America
http://horseshoepitching.com

JUMP ROPE

The Jump Rope Institute
703-580-6302
http://jumpropeinstitute.com

USA Jump Rope
936-295-3332
http://usajumprope.org

KICKBALL

DCKickball
DCK SPORTS LLC
http://dckickball.org

Mojo Kickball
http://mojokickball.com

World Adult Kickball Association
www.kickball.com

KUBB

Old Time Games
800-833-1448
www.oldtimegames.com

PlayKubb UK
info@kubb.co.uk
http://kubb.co.uk

LACROSSE

Federation of International Lacrosse
302-652-4530
www.filacrosse.com

Lacrosse Information
www.lacrosse-information.com

U.S. Lacrosse
410-235-6882
http://uslacrosse.org

LADDER TOSS

Ladder Golf Inc.
866-710-2582
http://laddergolf.com

Monkeyball
517-449-8256
http://playmonkeyball.com

MINIATURE GOLF

Big Birdie Golf
800-275-0591
http://bigbirdiegolf.com

Miniature Golf Association of the U.S.
817-738-3344
http://mgaus.org

Professional Miniature Golf Association
866-627-5233
http://thepmga.com

QOLF
BONFIT AMERICA
888-426-6348
http://qolf.com

MÖLKKY

www.molkkyusa.com
www.molkky.com

QUOITS

United States Quoiting Association
http://usqa.org

SACK RACING

Griffith Bag Company
800-433-2615
http://griffithbag.com

SEPAK TAKRAW

USA Takraw Association
info@takrawusa.com
http://takrawusa.com

TUG OF WAR

Tug of War International Federation
http://tugofwar-twif.org

United States Amateur Tug-of-War Association
800-884-6927
http://usatowa.com

VOLLEYBALL

International Fistball Association
www.ifa-fistball.com

United States Fistball Association
262-677-4254
http://usfistball.com

USA Volleyball
http://usavolleyball.org

Volleyball World Wide
volleyballorg@hotmail.com
http://volleyball.org

WIFFLE BALL

The Wiffle Ball, Inc.
203-924-4643
http://wiffle.com

Acknowledgments

As odd as it may be to first and foremost say thank you to a place and time, Vicki and I need to do that for Maine from the 1960s to now. We have both moved away, but without our mutual and lasting connection to the Pine Tree State's fields, forests, streams, lawns, and playgrounds of our youth, the spirit that brought this book to life might not have endured.

You don't make it through countless hours of fun and games without amazing memories of family and friends. For Victoria, Agatha Wooten Armstead's Forest Edge Farm nurtured her soul and laid the foundation for the joy she has brought to her own beautiful children, Maya and Jasper. For me, the outdoor adventures have moved from the dairy farm and Mom's backyard in Maine to Dad and Marny's backyard in Gloversville, New York, to a quarter-century of summer days and nights at the Lessels camp in Belmont, New Hampshire. Thank you, Jane, Uncle Allen, and Elaine for always making my family — Katie, Christina, Duke, Aimee, and Angie — feel like your family.

Beneath the joyful veneer that springs forth from this book, another reality must be addressed: children are not outside playing like they used to be, and that's a big problem. Physiologically and psychologically much is lost when children spend too much time in front of the computer, television, or other electronic devices. Our admiration and praise go to the research and outreach of Dr. Rhonda Clements and others involved with the International Play Association, which is dedicated to the advancement of real, unstructured free time for children.

We absolutely need to acknowledge Storey Publishing for its unwavering belief and patience. This project has been in the works for years; our busy careers might have otherwise derailed this great little book. So thank you, Pam Art, Dan Reynolds, and our editor, Lisa Hiley, for hanging in there and giving us the opportunity to relive our youth on these pages.

Finally, I want to thank my writing partner, the glorious Victoria Rowell, and her agent, Irene Webb, for jumping on board for this rollicking ride. In the midst of reading Hollywood scripts, shooting television pilots, and launching high-profile book tours, one of my all-time favorite actresses didn't laugh out loud when I asked her to help with a book about kubb, Mölkky, and Double Ball. "This is so intrinsic to family, fitness, nature, and togetherness," said Victoria. "Yes! I'd be honored." We've had an absolute blast.

— **P. T.**

Credits

Index

Page references in *italics* indicate illustrations
or photographs.

206

207

Other Storey Titles You Will Enjoy

Canine Sports & Games, by Kristin Mehus-Roe.
A full-range of fun, athletic activities — something for every dog and owner.
256 pages. Paper. ISBN 978-1-60342-083-9.

Catch the Wind, Harness the Sun, by Michael J. Caduto.
More than 20 exciting activities and experiments focused on renewable energy.
224 pages. Paper. ISBN 978-1-60342-794-4.
Hardcover. ISBN 978-7-60342-971-9.

The Nature Connection, by Clare Walker Leslie.
An interactive workbook packed with creative, year-round nature activities.
304 pages. Paper. ISBN 978-1-60342-531-5.

Nature's Art Box, by Laura C. Martin.
Cool projects for crafty kids to make with natural materials.
224 pages. Paper. ISBN 978-1-58017-490-9.

The Organic Lawn Care Manual, by Paul Tukey.
A comprehensive volume of natural lawn-care information to answer the growing
demand for organic grass.
272 pages. Paper. ISBN 978-1-58017-649-1.
Hardcover. ISBN 978-1-58017-655-2.

The Secret Lives of Backyard Bugs, by Judy Burris and Wayne Richards.
A one-of-a-kind look at amazing butterflies, moths, spiders, dragonflies, and
other insects.
136 pages. Paper. ISBN 978-1-60342-563-6.

These and other books from Storey Publishing are available
wherever quality books are sold or by calling 1-800-441-5700.
Visit us at *www.storey.com*.